MOTHERS

MOTHERS

Memories from Famous Daughters & Sons

Foreword by Líam Neeson

First published 1999 by The O'Brien Press Ltd.,
20 Victoria Road, Dublin 6, Ireland.
Tel. +353 1 4923333; Fax. +353 1 4922777
email: books@obrien.ie
website: www.obrien.ie
Reprinted 2000
Published in association with UNICEF Ireland

ISBN: 0-86278-605-3

British Library Cataloguing-in-publication Data
Malone, Niamh
Mothers : memories from famous daughters & sons
1.Mothers 2.Motherhood - Literary collections
I.Title
306.8'743

2 3 4 5 6 7 8 9
00 01 02 03 04 05 06

The O'Brien Press receives
assistance from

The Arts Council
An Chomhairle Ealaíon

Cover pictures by kind permission of: Macintosh and Otis, Inc., New York, John Davis Fine
Paintings/Bridgeman Art Library, London, Galerie La Vong, Hong Kong.

Layout and design: The O'Brien Press Ltd.
Colour separations: C&A Print Services Ltd.
Printing: MPG Books Ltd.

· CONTENTS ·

ABOUT UNICEF

UNICEF was created by the United Nations General Assembly in 1946 to meet the emergency needs of children in post-war Europe and China.

The work of UNICEF has changed greatly since that time. What has remained constant is its work for and on behalf of children throughout the world.

UNICEF now works in over 160 countries. All of these countries have a high incidence of infant and under-five mortality, that is, children who die before their first or fifth birthday. Usually poverty is a major cause of child death and disadvantage.

UNICEF remains committed to working for children by developing country programmes in the areas of Child Health and Nutrition, Water Supply and Sanitation, Education and Early Childhood Development. UNICEF also responds to children in emergency situations which are caused by war, natural disasters and famine.

For children in especially difficult circumstances, such as those involved with child labour and sexual exploitation, UNICEF runs special programmes which provide rehabilitation, and works to end these practices throughout the world.

Since it is a non-political organisation, UNICEF has been able to work with all sides in conflict situations to ensure early access to and assistance for children.

As part of its efforts to improve children's health and rights across the world, UNICEF campaigns and works to improve women's health. The inequity of women's lives means that of the 1.3 billion people living in poverty world-wide, more than 70% are girls and women.

For many women, this lifetime of disadvantage begins at birth and means that they are denied medical care to survive, education and nutrition to develop, and work long hours throughout their lives.

As estimated 585,000 women die each year during pregnancy or childbirth, and 300 million women live with permanent injuries or chronic disabilities due to complications of pregnancy or childbirth.

Nearly 99% of these deaths and injuries are in developing countries and most could be averted by ensuring women's access to effective maternal and child health care.

In Sub-Saharan Africa, the risk of death, related to maternal causes, is 250 times greater than that of a woman in Western Europe.

In industrialised countries almost all births occur under medical supervision, while in developing countries only 53% of births take place with a skilled birth attendant and only 40% in hospitals or clinics.

Girls aged fifteen to nineteen are twice as likely to die from childbirth as women in their twenties. Pregnancy-related complications are the main cause of death for girls of this age group world-wide.

It is therefore appropriate that the funds raised from this book *Mothers*, which includes the recollections of so many well-known people about their mothers, should benefit UNICEF Programmes for safe motherhood throughout the world.

INTRODUCTION

Hello. This is Líam Neeson, Special Patron of the Irish Committee for UNICEF, saying a warm 'Thank you' for supporting this very interesting project.

In my role as Special Patron, I try to help UNICEF highlight some of the issues which influence their work. This project is one of these.

Every day, UNICEF workers witness maternal and childhood mortalities as a result of hunger and disease, but also from complications of pregnancy and childbirth which could be easily avoided.

The funds raised from this important book will help to raise funds for UNICEF's Programmes for Safe Motherhood. Each of the contributors to this book has written a piece which reflects the influence their mother had on their life, or indeed the person who most represented mother to them. We asked them to write about their mothers because although UNICEF is a children's organisation, we also work with the primary carers of children, most often their mothers.

In compiling this book, we approached many people to participate, not only those included here. Many people we approached felt it was too difficult a task, to write about their mother, and so decided not to take part. Many of the final contributors said that this was one of the hardest things they had ever had to write. Perhaps this highlights how emotive the whole subject is. It also reinforces the importance of Safe Motherhood projects to try to lessen needless deaths of women and children around the world.

Our contributors have written very different accounts of their experiences, some positive, some negative, some prose, some poetry. This book, then, is a gathering of memories, which we hope will help to save lives and create memories for other families in the future.

I hope you enjoy it. Thank you for your support.

Liam Neeson

Líam Neeson

PRESIDENT MARY MCALEESE

President Mary McAleese was inaugurated President of Ireland in
1997. A distinguished barrister, President McAleese's
professional career has included appointment as Reid Professor
of Criminal Law, Trinity College, Dublin, Pro Vice Chancellor of
the Queens' University of Belfast and Director of the Institute of
Professional Legal Studies at the Queens' University of Belfast.
President McAleese has also been the recipient of honorary
degrees and fellowships from law and university establishments.
President McAleese and her husband Martin have three children
– Emma, Sara-Mai and Justin.

Extract from an address by President Mary McAleese on the occasion of the
UNICEF Mothers' Day Lunch 1998:

In 'commemorating motherhood', as we do every year on Mother's Day, we pause and reflect on our own circumstances and those of other mothers throughout the world. It is a time when we count our own blessings and good fortune, a time when we compare them with the 'blessings' that others endure – with the struggles, the obstacles, the good times and the bad.

As a start, though, we look for the common denominator in mothering and motherhood. All of us who are fortunate to be mothers know of the great desires and sense of duty that we have as home-keepers, educators, as nurses of children and as teachers of holy things – to do what is absolutely best for our children; to show them the way; to provide for them; to educate them; to protect them; to do right by them.

That duty and responsibility puts us all into the same category. We speak the same language, we share the same fears, we have the same hopes and desires for our children.

That role is summed up very well by Katherine Tynan, in her poem, 'Any Woman':

> At me the children warm their hands;
> I am their light of love alive
> Without me cold the hearthstone stands
> Nor could the precious children thrive

For many mothers, these duties, these dreams and hopes, cannot become a reality. For those for whom the provision of a basic existence for themselves and their families represents a dream – a dream which can seem unrealisable. The things that many of us take for granted – those natural aspirations for our children – are not even 'dreamt of' in their 'philosophy'. For many who are enslaved by domestic violence, alcoholism or illnesses, or who are bearing the brunt of civil conflict – these hopes and dreams seem so far from their reality. There are those too, who have to live with the pain and frustration of watching their children suffer from abuse and deprivation – those who are like, as St Matthew puts it, 'Rachel weeping for her children, and would not be comforted, because they are not'.

It is important too, to bear in mind that suffering and struggling of women is not confined to developing countries, or to places where there is conflict or disaster. In the towns and cities of the developed world, in the lanes and byways of modern economies, women also suffer from limited access to means and opportunity.

As we commemorate motherhood, we think of the great strides

that have been made over the last three decades, as reflected in the statistics for increased life expectancy, reduced child deaths, reduced malnutrition, and increased adult literacy in poor countries.

The impressive statistics, however, conceal the great imbalance that still exists in the distribution of the world's wealth, the burden on women who still do two-thirds of the world's work hours, receive a tenth of the world's income, own less than a hundredth of the world's property, and continue to face problems such as low life expectancy, high levels of infant, child and maternal mortality, limited access to safe water and sanitation, malnourished children and low literacy rates.

For the longer term, improving access to education for girls is the key to enabling more and more women to attain leadership positions at all levels of society. As the African proverb tells us, 'If we educate a boy, we educate one person. If we educate a girl, we educate a family and a whole nation.'

GERRY ADAMS

Gerry Adams is the President of Sinn Féin. He is fifty, married with one son. He was born in west Belfast, the eldest of ten children. He was the Member of Parliament for West Belfast from 1983 until 1992 and was re-elected in 1997. Gerry Adams began his political life in the 1960s as a founder member of the North of Ireland Civil Rights Movement. He has been imprisoned on a number of occasions and was shot five times in a loyalist murder bid in 1984. With SDLP leader John Hume, he kickstarted the current peace process and led Sinn Féin through the negotiations which resulted in the Good Friday Agreement. Gerry Adams is an accomplished author with eight books to his credit, including Before the Dawn, An Irish Voice *and* The Street and Other Stories.

My mother died on the fourth of September 1992. She was sixty-seven years old. She died suddenly after a huge stroke. Her life was filled with stress and her health was never the best but her going was so unexpected that even yet, at a certain emotional level, it is hard to come to terms with her non-presence.

I am her oldest child. I pause after the word *child* and I smile that I describe myself thus. But that is what I am. When all else is stripped away or set aside that is what all of us are. Somebody's child. My mother had thirteen children. Three of us died at birth – three little boys. Our Seán's twin brother Brendan and two other brothers, twins also, Séamus and David. The rest of us survived. Five brothers and five sisters. My mother gave life to and for every one of us.

Her name was Annie. When I was born she was twenty-three. A child came every year after that. I don't know how she coped. We were poor. Not *Angela's Ashes* poor, because we had the support of loving grandmothers and a wider family circle to sustain us. But we were poor nonetheless. So was everyone else. Or everyone we knew. That's probably why we children never noticed it at the time.

My mother carried our family. She was of that generation of Irish people in which the man of the house provided the wages if he was lucky enough to be in work, and the woman of the house did the rest. It wasn't fair. And then when the ten of us started to move out, the grandchildren started to move in and the cycle started again.

My Ma loved dancing. Céilí and old time were her favourites. She had a terrific sweet tooth. She read a lot, as did many of her generation, and she sang around the house all the time. Well, most of the time. All of these habits I have inherited from her, although my singing is not as good and I don't know one whole song right through.

I may have inherited other habits or traits. I hope so. Some day I must take time to find out. But one thing my mother gave to me without being conscious of it, and that is a deep appreciation of the unselfish, unconditional and undying nature of mother love. And what mothers put up with.

I told her that a few times over the years. Half joking. And serious as well. At set times or when I was in a mood. But when she died I wasn't with her.

She was rushed suddenly to the City Hospital in Belfast. All of our family gathered at her bedside, including our Seán who was released from prison, handcuffed to a prison officer. I was nervous about going.

Not for myself because I could have gone and returned from the hospital quite quickly. If there was danger – and 1992 was a dangerous year – it would have been for those who were staying. So I didn't go. I don't regret that. It was the prudent thing to do. My Ma would have understood. But I am sorry I didn't get to tell Annie Adams just how much I love her.

So thanks Ma. Tá mé buíoch duitse.

Bertie Ahern

Bertie Ahern TD was elected Taoiseach on 26 June 1997. He has been leader of the Fianna Fáil Party since 1994. The Taoiseach has held a number of offices in previous Governments, including Minister for Finance, Minister for Labour and Government Chief Whip. He has been a member of Dáil Éireann since 1977, representing his native Dublin.

Who says there is no spirit,
When I know you're always there,
Watching all I do and every day
Thinking those warm mother thoughts
That no one else can share.
The life I breathe is breath of yours,
The heart I feel is your love too
And when I see, it is to great degree
How you and Da would like me to.
Sing, soft Julia, for me just like you did
When boyhood dreams were full of bliss,
I miss and miss the need to see you
In your quiet home where for so long
You were My Ma, with Da, and us.

Bertie Ahern

DARINA ALLEN

Darina Allen owns and runs the internationally renowned Ballymaloe Cookery School at Shanagarry, County Cork, with her husband, Tim Allen. The school and gardens attract visitors from all over the world. Since 1989, she has presented eight series of her television cookery programme, Simply Delicious, *all with accompanying cookbooks. Darina's other prize-winning publications include* Traditional Irish Cooking *and* A Year at Ballymaloe Cookery School. *Along with contributing regularly to many publications, Darina has been featured on television in Britain and the United States.*

When I close my eyes I can still smell the great big tray of golden scones with crunchy sugary tops, just coming out of the oven. As I ran up the hill from the village school, I'd try to guess what Mummy might have for a treat today. Maybe it was the fresh brown bread that she baked every day in big triangles with some honey, or maybe she'd had time to make little buns. Would she have waited for me to come home to help to ice them? Was there raspberry jam still left? We could make some into butterfly buns and ice the others with white icing and decorate with shiny red cherries and little diamonds of angelica. Problem was how to stop the boys stealing them before the icing was set – I can still hear them squabbling!

All of my earliest childhood memories are tied up with food.

Because there were nine of us there was always something bubbling on the stove, cooling on the window sill, baking in the oven. My siblings and I learned to cook by 'osmosis'. When I was just tall enough to see over the table top, Mummy would give me a little piece of bread dough to make into a little cistín. She'd show me how to handle it gently so as not to make it heavy, and consequently I learned how to make bread, like so many other things, without ever realising it could be difficult. She taught me how to judge the heat of the oven with my hand, how to decide when the milk from our Kerry cow was sour enough for soda bread, how a blob of sour cream would always lighten the texture of bread and scones.

I took all this for granted, it was simply part of every day. When the wild mushrooms appeared in the fields, she'd stew them in milk – a flavour I'll never forget. When we collected baskets of damsons from the fields beside the castle, she'd make them into damson jam. We'd help to skim off the stones as they rose to the top of the pot and then cover the pots. My mother's damson jam was famous at the Dominican Convent in Wicklow where I spent five years as a boarder – it greatly enhanced my popularity at tea time, when the most toffee-nosed girls would jostle each other to sit beside me just to taste the jam.

From Mummy I also learned how to sew, knit and even embroider. She sowed the first seeds of my love for gardening and my fascination with poultry. When I was little, and God knows where she found the time, she smocked the bodices of my summer dresses and knitted me fluffy little angora boleros that made me feel a hundred dollars. She was, and still is, a wonderful housekeeper. Every spring, the entire house was spring cleaned from top to bottom, and summer curtains and bedspreads replaced the heavier winter ones. As the weather improved, we looked forward to the day we would be allowed to shed our winter woollies and unpack the trunks of summer clothes.

Mummy seemed almost effortlessly to create a home that was warm and secure, where we felt safe and loved. We grew in confidence and learned by example the values by which we now live our lives. It all seems calm and natural although I now know that she felt utterly overwhelmed when she was widowed at just thirty-six from my father whom she adored. She was left with nine children under fourteen years of age, one of whom was born a month after my father's death. Yet she gradually picked up the pieces and started to learn the business, something she'd never had to concern herself with before. Her beautiful rich brown hair turned silvery-grey almost overnight but, despite her loneliness, she got on with the business of rearing and educating us and eventually took up golf and bridge which have given her much pleasure ever since. When, at just twenty years of age, Tim and I announced our intention to marry, despite her deep religious convictions she supported us resolutely in our efforts to secure the many dispensations needed for a Roman Catholic to marry a Quaker, and supported our right to have two ceremonies, something unheard of up to then. This was a brave stand to take in the late sixties in a country village where the rules of the church were not traditionally questioned. This support meant so much to us, I shall always be grateful for it.

In recent years, Mummy has been able to relax and enjoy a little more free time, enjoy her leisure and travel more. She loves to walk and is happiest scaling the peaks of the Comeragh mountains in West Waterford with her family and grandchildren, all of whom now live in Ireland, to her great joy. An inspirational woman – I'm so proud to call her mother.

Darina Allen

Mary Banotti

*Named European of the Year in 1997, Mary Banotti
has been a Member of the European Parliament since 1994.
She was a Presidential candidate in the 1997
Irish Presidential campaign.*

My memories of my mother are generally very sharp, but I have difficulty separating the real memories from the emotional reaction evoked by seeing photographs of her as a younger woman with her children, generally on Dollymount Strand. Family photographs of that era – the forties – generally tended to centre around the one annual picnic to the beach, First Communions or birthday parties, and in all of those she's a handsome, good-looking woman, with her sleeves rolled up, competent in dealing with her children and very happy.

She was widowed in 1949 at the age of thirty-eight, with six children under the age of ten. I was the eldest, at ten years of age. As the eldest in the family I was probably more directly affected by her grief and sorrows at the time. Clearly she missed our father quite terribly. She went back to work as a Domestic Science teacher at Cathal Brugha Street College of Catering, and it wasn't until thirty years later that we as her children began to realise how much she actually enjoyed her work and her involvement with her students. She clearly made a significant impact on them, as to this day we continue to meet people who she taught and who remark on the affect she had on their lives. She was also a feminist before her time, believing passionately that, in the catering industry, the female students were just as capable of becoming great chefs as the men.

She had had a very difficult childhood and her family was greatly affected by the War of Independence and the Civil War and the impact of the death of Michael Collins, her uncle, on the entire family. For this reason, she found it difficult to be a relaxed hostess, probably having realised from an early age that people who came to the house were not necessarily coming for fun, but rather for shelter and safety. As children I know they were always warned not to speak about anybody who visited their house. She had very ambiguous feelings about politics, associating it inevitably with loss and grief and fear. How ironic, for somebody with such feelings about political life, that two of her daughters ended up in public life. She continued to have the most fearful anxieties about our capacity to deal with the rough and tumble of our public offices.

She enjoyed the first ten years of her retirement, playing golf and bridge and even doing a little bit of travel, but in the last ten years of her life she was severely afflicted by Parkinson's Disease. I always felt it was the most awful irony for a person who always believed that most problems in life could be solved by a 'quick walk around the block', that for the last years of her life the one thing that she could not do was take a quick walk around the block.

She held court in Our Lady's Manor in Dalkey from 1989 to the time of her death in 1997. All the qualities that had infused her life – courage, passionate attention to duty and resilience – were present right to the end of her life. She exercised significant control over all of us right up to the moment she died, surrounded by her family. She was ready to go when she finally died, having, through her family and through her work as an educator, influenced the lives of a vast number of people. Her funeral was enormously moving, and in a sense also became a celebration of the contribution that many of the widows in Ireland have made, not only to their own families but to the communities in which they lived.

MAEVE BINCHY

Maeve Binchy has been a teacher and journalist, but is best-known as a novelist. Her books have been translated into more than twenty languages and made into films and television series. She is married to the writer Gordon Snell and lives in Dalkey, County Dublin, close to where she grew up.

My Mother died in 1967 but in many ways I truly and honestly think that she is still alive. I can almost see her throwing her eyes up to heaven about the many awful things that I do, like stapling up a hem because I can't sew it, or having to take the empty wine bottles separately to three different bottle banks after a party.

But mainly I think of her when I am nervous, and the very memory gives me huge confidence. If I have to stand up before a large crowd and my stomach turns to water, I just imagine her telling me to hold my shoulders back and to remember that most of them just want to go home for their tea so make it short. And then I'm fine.

'We are as good as any of them,' she used to say. I'm not quite sure who They were or who We were but I knew we were all equals whatever we were.

I knew the things we were NOT, like we were not thin and beautiful, or very rich, or very poor, or any kind of Society. But I knew we were fine so that was a really good start. And my mother was someone who could remove fish bones from peoples' throats, plant gardens in terrible soil and dress four children in times of recession, without the luxury of emigrant cousins sending us clothes parcels.

She was a big, joyful woman, who in theory should have married a man who went to the races and the Casino and drank after hours. Instead she fell for and married my father, a quiet, bookish lawyer, who loved her with that total devotion that gave us all such a secure and happy childhood.

She made most of the decisions at home, like where we would all go to school, and if we would build an outside lavatory, and whether there would be enough money for us to rent a house for the month of August in Ballybunion in County Kerry.

She had been very beautiful when she was young. I know that from old pictures, but she had changed any kind of smart lifestyle that she once had in order to look after her four children, and from then on she seemed to wear a big woolly cardigan with huge pockets for gardening tools while she grew roses and fuchsias and lilacs to give us a colourful background as we grew up.

It's hard for one member of a family to describe a mother, because obviously she belonged to all of us, so we all have different stories to tell. There is an album of black-and-white pictures, where she held us all in turn as babies, pride glowing like a light from her face. And as well as snapshots, there are a thousand stories to remember.

Like the time the hens died of old age, like real old age, and she brought their bodies in on the bus to the Department of Agriculture in case it was Fowl Pest and we might get compensation.

Like the times she would stop strangers in the streets to tell them that we had passed exams. Like the night I was going to my first dance, and she told me I would take the sight out of their eyes. It wasn't anywhere approaching the truth, nor was it borne out by my success on the dance floor, but it's a wonderful memory.

Every child in the world should have a mother who can say something like that.

JOHN BOORMAN

John Boorman was born in London, but has lived in Ireland for more than thirty years. His film-making career, spanning three decades, includes such films as The General, *which was awarded Best Director at the Cannes Film Festival 1998;* Two Nudes Bathing; Beyond Rangoon; I Dreamt I Woke Up; Where The Heart Is; Hope And Glory, *which received five Oscar nominations in 1987;* The Emerald Forest, *the making of which was documented in his book* Money Into Light; Excalibur; Exorcist II: The Heretic; Zardoz; Deliverance, *which received three Oscar nominations in 1972;* Leo The Last, *which was awarded Best Director at the Cannes Film Festival 1970;* Hell in The Pacific; Point Blank; *and his directorial debut in 1965,* Catch Us If You Can. *His annual film publication,* Projections, *written with co-editor Walter Donohue, is now in its ninth year.*

Excerpt from **Hope and Glory,** *an account of my childhood during the Second World War:*

My father and his friend Mac had recently been de-mobbed from the army after the Great War. My father had a job, but poor Mac just could not find one, even though he had left the army earlier than George. Most of their school friends had been killed in action, so George and Mac stuck together, were never apart. Word reached them that the new landlord of the Alexander Hotel at the foot of Wimbledon

Hill had four beautiful daughters. When they got there, it was jam-packed with young fellows come to worship at the shrine. Henry Chapman, eventually to become my Grandfather, had thoughtfully covered the walls behind the bars in mirrors. Only three of the daughters were in evidence, Bobby being still too young, but the reflections suggested an infinity of loveliness. They were innocent, demure. As George and Mac downed their pints of mild and bitter, swooning in that delirium of delight, they both fell in love with Ivy, the eldest of the Chapman girls.

George and Mac courted Ivy, took her out, were invited to the bungalow on the Thames at Shepperton that Grandpa Chapman kept as his weekend retreat. She was attracted to them both. She found it hard to separate them in her heart. Her father glowered disapproval. Neither was grand enough for his beautiful daughter. Just penniless opportunists, he told Ivy, but she was inclined to escape her overbearing and tyrannical father.

My mother's affections began to veer towards Mac, but Mac still had no job and so could make no offer. He loved her deeply, but felt obliged to step back and give his friend George a clear field. My father would turn up at Shepperton without him. George made the running and Ivy waited in vain for Mac to declare himself.

Meanwhile, Grandpa was doing his best to marry off his daughters to better men. He took them all off to Ascot, completing his party with the Mayor of Wimbledon and other dignitaries.

It was the 1920s. George took Ivy to the *Danse de Thé* where her eyes would search for Mac, who was never there. Mother and her sisters were great exponents of the Charleston. Above and beyond all this was their passion for river life and their utter contempt for stuffy conventional living.

After giving a lavish wedding, Grandpa would have nothing more to do with George and Ivy, and certainly did not alleviate their poverty.

Father toiled at the clerical job he hated. Mother pined for the river; my father's pleasure was the sea.

My mother found herself trapped in a suburban street, exiled from her beloved Thames and married to a man she was deeply fond of, but did not love. The friendly bombs fell and she gathered up her children and fled to Shepperton. My father begged his friend Mac to watch over his young family.

My father had lived a twenty-year hangover from the intoxication of his Indian Army days. Although he was nearly forty, he could not wait to join up. It was blessed escape from the drudgery of his clerical job and perhaps from vague and unformed dissatisfactions with his marriage and his street.

My mother did part-time war work at Mac's factory. He was now an important man in a reserved occupation. He had a petrol allowance, and used to drive her home each afternoon. He would park his car in front of our bungalow and I would see them talking, mute behind the glass, their long-dormant love blossoming.

After my father died, my mother sold up and went to live in a flat facing the Thames at Kingston. She lived there with her sister Jenny and just around the corner from the other two, Bobby and Billy. Mother was the eldest. They all buried their husbands except Jenny, who spurned the institution of marriage. They loved to picnic by the river in their many favourite places that recall girlish escapades. On a warm day, they would still slip into the water and swim across and back.

In the film, I called my mother Grace, for that was the virtue she had in abundance. She died two years ago at the age of ninety-six.

Archbishop Seán Brady

*Born in County Cavan in 1939, Archbishop Seán Brady
has been Catholic Archbishop of Armagh and Primate of
All Ireland since 1996.*

Mothers, it is said, are the only people who never forget that you exist. Whether you have done good or bad, or whether you are famous or forgotten, ignored or revered, you can still be sure that in your mother's heart you are foremost. Whether it be food or formation, care or career, sponsor or spouse, only the best is good enough for their son or daughter.

Our mother was always working and, like many of her generation and background, she was a great respecter of the value of work. The financial benefits that accrued from her raising chickens or tending pet lambs were often problematic – to say the least – but my mother never turned away from it. Life was valuable, and whatever was in her care, be it animal or human, got her undivided attention.

She was an infinitely generous woman – with her time, her energy and her money. Indeed, this generosity was not always countenanced by us, her children, particularly when she insisted on sharing with outsiders our Christmas dinner, modest and all as that was in the rural Cavan of the 1950s! Again, I remember her generous response to people in distress. Her response was always instant and unquestioning.

We are sometimes at a loss to be specific about the virtues of someone taken so much for granted – the way all mothers are! But I ask myself whether I am always good-humoured, accommodating, interested in the careers of others? This is what she was, never moody or unpredictable or selfish. She wasn't a martyr either, but a strong-minded and assertive woman who had a good self-image and sought to inculcate that in her children. When I was appointed to the See of Armagh, a question I was asked was: 'What would your mother say?' I realised she would most probably reply: 'You have been chosen, give it your best, you can do it.' Mother never balked at anything; she expected nothing less from her children.

Mother was nothing if not courageous and that, together with her devotion to duty and generosity of heart, are the qualities that I would most like to emulate. Patrick Kavanagh's poem, 'In Memory of My Mother', expressed something of what is true of all mothers but particularly that courageous, hardworking, stoical, faith-filled people who stemmed from and toiled in the rough and inhospitable drumlins of Cavan and Monaghan:

> I do not think of you lying in the wet clay
> Of a Monaghan graveyard; I see
> You walking down a lane among the poplars
> On your way to the station, or happily
>
> Going to second Mass on a summer Sunday –
> You meet me and you say:
> 'Don't forget to see about the cattle –'

There was the lighter side to Mother too – her lively sense of humour, her avid interest in reading. I always remember the amazement of another Seán Brady, who visited Cavan and her in the 1980s, looking for his roots. He was charmed by her genuine welcome and hospitality and her ability to discuss Jane Austen. She could be frustrating too, in her irrational attachment to long-obsolete pieces of furniture, and if one might not call her prejudiced, she certainly could be opinionated.

Archbishop Seán Brady

VINCENT BROWNE

Vincent Browne was born in County Limerick in 1944. An economics and politics graduate, he began his career working for RTÉ, the Irish television and radio company. He covered the Soviet Invasion of Czechoslovakia for the Irish Times *newspaper in 1968. In the 1970s, he edited a publication called* Nusuight, *was Northern Editor of the* Irish Press *and worked at Independent Newspapers. In 1977, he co-founded Ireland's political and current affairs magazine,* Magill. *In 1983, he re-launched the* Sunday Tribune, *which he edited until 1994. He now works as a columnist with the* Irish Times, *presents a weeknight radio programme on RTÉ and works as a barrister since being called to the Bar in 1997.*

My mother died of Alzheimer's disease in January 1987. She had gone into deepening confusion over the previous two years, but until late October of the previous year she appeared physically healthy. Then, in late October, we were summoned home to Broadford, County Limerick, and on entering the house I realised she was going to die soon.

Several of us sat around the kitchen table with her. She was hopelessly confused. After an hour or so, the others had left the kitchen and she walked around behind me and put her hand on my shoulder. She said she wanted to say something to me and to listen to her because she would not be able to retain conversation beyond a minute or so.

She said she knew she would die soon and she wanted to say to me for the last time that she loved me. She said how she had worried for years about my abandonment of religion but how she had by then come to terms with that, knowing that I was trying to live my life to my beliefs. Then, with absolute clarity, she spoke about others we were close to and got me to make specific promises in relation to them. She said again that she loved me and immediately reverted to confusion. She never again spoke a sensible word to me.

Vincent Browne

I need to remember nothing else about her than that scene to recall her personality and character: loving, utterly selfless, reconciled to the fate that God had ordained for her. I don't think she had a very fulfilled life, and that was entirely because of how society treated women from the 1920s to the 1960s.

She was born in Glasgow to County Monaghan parents. Her father was killed in an accident when she was an infant, and her mother brought her and her two brothers and sister back to Ballybay, where the family lived in considerable hardship. She won a scholarship to St Louis Convent, Monaghan, and from there to UCC. There she did a degree through Irish in science, and then went on to do an MA in science, again through Irish. She returned to St Louis Convent, Monaghan, to teach and was there until she got married, about twelve years later.

She left her home and friends to set up a new home in Broadford, County Limerick. For several years, she was terribly lonely and, by the convention of those times, was precluded from continuing to work as a teacher. My father, sister, brothers and I became the centre of her life, along with her religious devotion. She was terribly ambitious for us, and particularly for me as the eldest son. At times the pressure she exerted was a little overpowering, but it was underlain with love, although that too was overpowering at times.

Like most mothers of her era, she lived life through her husband and children, instead of directly through herself. She would have loved it if I had got a 'proper job' – been a doctor or architect or even a barrister – but she was proud of my minor accomplishments, as she was of those of my sister and brothers.

I don't think she ever knew how I reciprocated her love and I am certain she would be amazed at how much I miss her.

JANE CLARE

*Born in Dublin, the youngest of four children, Jane Clare
is married to psychiatrist Anthony Clare. A BA in English
Literature and MA in Old and Middle English Literature, Jane
Clare is a part-time journalist and writer (*What Will I Be *was
published in 1995). She is a full-time mother of seven.*

My mother, Sheila Boland, was born on Good Friday, 13 April.
An inauspicious start to her life, she would reflect in later
years. She was a woman of many conjectures and varied opinions, the
poorest of which she reserved for the male of the species.

'Men!' she would say in tones of exasperation, more often than not
on the way home from Sunday Mass, 'What do they really know
about?' In her view, there was man's world, and there was reality. Reality was where women lived.

It was not just my father's ineptitude with anything practical
('Men' and 'Sarsfield', my father's name, were totally interchangeable
terms), or the regular sermons on sex, marriage and the family trum-
peted from the pulpit by celibate priests, that got on her nerves. It was
the system that was fraudulent. Men postured and pontificated, and
played political games, rugby games and war games by turn, while
women bore and reared their children, created and maintained homes,
fed and clothed the family, cared for the elderly relatives, managed the

household income and embraced these varied activities with the essence of life – that emotional output of love.

My mother was a feminist without portfolio. Perhaps because her secure childhood was shattered by the death of her father when she was twelve, she did not underrate the value of domesticity. Her mother, to support the family of three, trained to be a masseuse and ran a boarding house at the same time. In due course, she became masseuse to the Irish Army at St Bricin's Hospital. There was no time for home life. The two boys were educated, in accountancy and medicine. My mother left school and went to work in the civil service, where she met and, at the age of twenty-one, married my father, Sarsfield Hogan.

Her cumulative experience, of a mother too busy for affectionate gestures and of a truncated education, caused her on the one hand to regard working mothers with a jaundiced eye, and on the other to insist that her daughters must have the same educational opportunities as her sons. This apparent contradiction was based on a deep-seated sense of injustice to women and children alike.

She attacked her life with energy and commitment, even in its more difficult and unhappy moments. Apart from the family, friendship was her most valued resource. She was immensely sociable, charming and funny. She was also beautiful and multi-talented. She knitted, crocheted and sewed all the household furnishings, as well as her own and our clothes, all to professional standards. From christening robe to wedding dress, nothing was beyond her capabilities. Our home was an extension of her personality. Filled with lovely things acquired over the years by scrimping and saving on the housekeeping allowance, it remained a warm and welcoming place for friends, children and grandchildren until shortly before her death.

But the *pièce de résistance* was her garden. Gardening, from planning to execution, released her most creative instincts and abilities.

The results of her efforts gave her a rare sense of pride, for in the main her belief in the intrinsic worth of women did not translate into self-esteem. Moreover, gardening was the one area where men might be regarded as the equal of women. After all, anyone who shared her passion, and could grip a hoe, had to have a grip on Reality!

BILL CULLEN

Bill Cullen was born into poverty in Dublin's inner city. One of fourteen children, he spent most of his childhood selling fruit and newspapers on the city streets with his mother. He started working as a messenger boy in 1957 in a Ford dealership, and twelve years later was appointed Managing Director. Now his company, the Glencullen Motor Group, has an annual turnover of IR£250 million. He is also Chairman of the Children's Hour and Chairman of the Irish Youth Foundation, an organisation that raises money every year for disadvantaged youth.

I am from a family of fourteen children, born in a poverty-stricken inner-city Dublin tenement. Our family was raised in one large room, in a building housing more than one hundred men, women and children, with no water or electricity facilities. As the eldest boy, I became my mother's '*aide de camp*' at the tender age of five – helping her sell apples and fruit from her trader's stall on a Dublin street just after the war. It was a struggle for survival in those tough times, and my mother Mary taught me the skills of buying, selling and negotiating. She also gave me the invaluable gifts of self-confidence and integrity. Two of her many wise sayings were, 'You are as good as any man you'll ever meet', and, 'Your health and your good name are your most precious possessions'.

My mother was my mentor, my supporter and my guiding light. The words I spoke at her funeral expressed just a fraction of what she meant to me and barely scratched the surface of the depth of my appreciation for the fact that she was *my mother*:

Mary Cullen née Darcy, 1913–1986:
'Did you ever know that you're my hero?'

Mary Darcy's dynamic energy made her a born leader. She was reared in Dublin's troubled times, when the Irish Civil War raged and the Black-and-Tans dashed through the streets in their Crossley tenders. She raised a family of seven sons and seven daughters in the tough inner-city area around Seán McDermott Street. Mary sold fruit from a barrow opposite Argots in Henry Street, and her husband, Billy Culled, worked in Brooks Thomas on the North Wall docks.

For Mary every day was a non-stop affair, from morning mass at 6.00am through a twenty-hour day until 2.00am bedtime. Raising a large family as a full-time worker was tough going, but Mary made it look easy. I will cherish many memories of those days in Henry Street – cajoling the late evening customers to take the last few apples at knock-down prices; Mary dashing into the kitchen to get the fry ready for 'himself's' dinner with steam rising from her clothes, which were soaked from the day's downpour; the magnificence of her defiance in defending the elderly neighbours against a bullying rent collector, with an oratorial ability that Jim Larkin would have been proud of; Mary sitting at the table in the wee small hours, with the entire houschold fast asleep, and she with a sackful of socks, pullovers and gansies to be stitched and mended; and Mary in the mother's role, singing lullabies to the ever-present babies, while she cooked, washed and ironed all at the same time.

Mary Darcy sailed through more crises in one year than most

people will experience in a lifetime. Yet she was always there to handle the problems of the neighbourhood – 'If you want something done, ask a busy person'.

Mary Darcy's death at the age of seventy-three was unexpected. For me, it was unbelievable that such a human dynamo could just falter and stop. I thought she was indestructible, but the good Lord knew that she carried too many burdens, for too long, and gave her the reward of Eternal Life.

Her family will grieve – for Mary, yes, but more for ourselves in being deprived of her presence, her example and her love. We will grieve and be sad that we didn't give her more; that we didn't acknowledge our massive debt to her; that we didn't tell her how much we loved her and appreciated all she had suffered for our sakes. Thank God every one of us has some of her character and will have the strength to live our lives in the way Mary taught us.

'I can fly higher than an eagle,
You are the wind beneath my wings.'

Despite, or because of, my humble background, I became one of Ireland's entrepreneurial success stories – today, I am Chairman and owner of the Glencullen Motor Group, with an annual turnover of IR£250 million pounds. A direct result of my mother's teaching, because survival is the mainstay of the business world and Mary was an expert survivor.

I still remember my roots and am also the driving force behind the Irish Youth Foundation, which raises IR£600,000 annually for projects to help disadvantaged youth countrywide.

I hope our Mam is proud and glad of those things I have already achieved and those I have yet to.

Bill Cullen

The Most Reverend Dr Robin Eames

Archbishop Robin Eames has been Anglican Archbishop of Armagh and Primate of All Ireland since 1986. A writer and broadcaster, he has had a long-term involvement in the Northern Ireland Peace Process.

It is not possible for anyone to put into a few words the influence over their life of a mother. Glimpses of childhood, memories of home, family gatherings, words and actions, pain and joy, hopes realised and hopes disappointed ... they all come back when in later life one tries to think of a mother.

In my case it will always be a sense of overwhelming love and gratitude, but also of respect. I enjoyed the happiest of childhoods in a home where love did not have to be spoken – it was there all the time, unspoken at times, but a part of the air we breathed. At its centre was my mother. Her very presence spoke of security, love and understanding. Prompting, cautioning, encouraging – and, while at times keeping her thoughts to herself, providing me with a set of values which despite many failings I have found to influence me as an adult. Values of compassion, caring, duty and loyalty. Values of listening and values which, perhaps without realising it, I hope I have passed on to my own sons.

The Christian faith lay at the centre of my childhood home. My mother practised that faith as well as simply believing in it. My decision to be ordained had so much to do with the influence of my late father; the strength to examine my vocation came from my mother.

Gratitude for a mother is one thing. Thankfulness goes much further. I thank God for His great gift to me of a mother who, when I needed her most, seemed to be 'always there'.

Archbishop Robin Eames

DESMOND FITZGERALD

Desmond Fitzgerald, the Knight of Glin, is President of the Irish Georgian Society and representative for Christie's auctioneers in Ireland. He is the author and co-author of many books and articles on Irish paintings, furniture and architectural and garden history. A Fellow of the Society of Antiquaries and Member of the Royal Institute of Architects of Ireland, he runs a historic country-house hotel at his home, Glin Castle, County Limerick.

The nursery at Glin was on the third floor, facing west across the courtyard and the long wing of the house and beyond to the shimmering Shannon, with Tarbert Lighthouse like a little white exclamation mark in the distance – at night it blinked on and off in a comfortingly familiar way. The top floor consisted of the nursery, the night nursery, a very spartan bathroom and two small bedrooms for my two older sisters.

The nursery was painted, like much of Glin in those days, an inevitable cream, with the coved ceilings white. At teatime, heralded by the smell of a Balkan Sobranie Turkish cigarette, my mother appeared. Tea and toast by the fire with my mother and Nanny Reay were the high point of the day, after disagreeable lessons from a primer called *Reading Without Tears* (though there were many of them). It was Una, the nursery maid and later the loyal family general factotum, who really brought me up, and it was her quiet but firm influence which taught me to read, 'rite and haltingly attempt 'rithmetic.

My mother was a tall, elegant woman with a straight nose and a fine oval face. She was a beauty. When she first married into Glin in 1929 the locals, who were farmers to the man, made the comment, 'Ah sure, doesn't she have a fine fall for her water', which translated as, 'Doesn't she have a fine pair of long legs'!

She fell in love with Glin, with its neo-classical ceilings, flying staircase and romantic Shannon-side park. My parents didn't have much money, but my mother used to make weekly expeditions with Eva Dunraven to Mr Coleman's Patrick Street antique shop in Limerick. She collected some handsome pieces of mahogany, prints, watercolours and bric-a-brac to furnish Glin, which had lost so many of its contents after a bankruptcy sale in 1803, just after the house was built.

My meticulous father, whose main interest was motorcars, ran the farm and the salmon fishery. Sadly, he developed TB. My parents travelled abroad in the 1940s to the United States and Switzerland to find a cure, but he died young in 1949, and my mother was left with three children and very little money. She took over the running of the farm.

The early 1950s saw her taking in paying guests and struggling against all odds. Even in the darkest days, she indulged my budding artistic interests by buying two splendid 18th-century chimneyplaces to decorate the dining and smoking rooms when she certainly could not afford them. She and her family loved furniture and beautiful things, and it was her keen visual sense which made her fight so hard and determinedly to save the place when there seemed very little future for it.

However, life soon changed for the better. By happy chance my mother and father had met Ray Milner, a charming Canadian in the oil and gas business, on a train to Chicago when they were on their way to

Arizona, whose dry climate was considered curative for my father's TB. They always kept in touch and, to cut a long story short, my mother married Ray in 1954. Glin wove a spell over him, so he restored it from top to bottom in the late 1950s when labour was cheap. Glin was revitalised by my mother and new step-father.

It is often the women who keep old houses going. This was certainly the case from 1929, when my mother first came to distant Glin, to the time she was widowed again in the 1970s. At this point, my wife and I took up the gauntlet and have turned Glin Castle into a romantic historic-house hotel.

My mother's strength and bravery saved an Irish country house from the usual dismal and decaying fate of so many others, whose ruins still dot the Irish landscape.

I thank her for her efforts.

Mrs Veronica Milner passed away on 5 November 1998, after a short illness following an operation.

PÁDRAIG FLYNN

*Pádraig Flynn has worked in the teaching profession and was
also a self-employed businessman for a time. He began his
political career in 1967 as an elected member of Mayo County
Council for the Fianna Fáil party. He was first elected to the Dáil
in 1977, and had a very successful parliamentary career, holding
six ministerial positions. He has been a member of the European
Commission since 1993, when he was responsible for the Justice,
Immigration and Home Affairs portfolio. From 1993, he also had
responsibility for the Employment, Industrial Relations and
Social Affairs portfolio.*

When someone asks me about my mother, it stills me, no matter
how busy I am. I can instantly see, but not convey, the power
of the big woman she was, strong in mind and body.

She was before her time, my mother. She worked outside the home
all her life. She set up her own business at a time when women were not
expected to be entrepreneurs. She drove at a time when relatively few
women owned cars. She worked – and played golf – with stamina.
Strength. And she had many skills.

Such skill was in those gifted hands. She was a costumier. You
could present her with a photographed garment from the most recent
French collection and she could reproduce it in every cut, finish and
fold, with nothing more than a look at the picture. Her capacity to

visualise and then translate into cloth her understanding of a design was unique. Good taste was part of it, as was an understanding of the characteristics of every fabric and every blend of fabrics.

Creativity, as she saw it, came after skill. When I was growing up, it was a message hammered home again and again. It didn't matter whether it was Irish dancing you wanted to do or music; tennis you wanted to play, or golf – the first step was to learn the correct methods. There was no grabbing a golf stick or a tennis racquet and flailing away; we learned how to hold the implement, how and where to stand, what the rules were and which were the protocols, and we learned them first. Do it right was the recurring message. Learn to do it right. She invested in skill-training for us, and in the process built up in us a respect for consistency and discipline and practise. A lucky fluke might be fun, but doing something right was much more important. You could be proud of something achieved by persistent, committed hard work.

She was always a proud woman. Proud of her family. Proud of her capacity to give 100% and then a little bit more, whether to us or to someone who needed some help. The pride was evident, but never boasted about. There were community and charity tasks to be undertaken with the same energy given to work or sport. They were not talked about. To talk about something like that would have been a smallness, and there was none of that in her. There were jobs to be done, to ensure that everybody had the chance of a better life, and she would do those jobs. If she had a bias, it was toward her own. Her own children would have every opportunity to have a better life than she had, every chance to fulfil the potential she saw in them. Above all else, she had a big, soft, loving heart when it came to her children and her grandchildren. She was a good mother in all things and had enormous, simple devotion and faith.

So it is that to this day, when one of us completes a task, overcomes an obstacle or is honoured with an award, the first instinct is to wish that she could see it, because she has ownership in it.

There is a great place in my heart and my memory for her – and it grows greater by the year.

MAY FRISBY

*May Frisby was born in Kilkenny, the fourth of ten children,
to publicans Lily and Michael Frisby. She opened her first
business, Shrimps wine bar, in Dublin in 1982, and then
introduced fresh pasta to Ireland with her outstanding success,
the Pasta Fresca restaurant in Chatham Street, Dublin, in 1985.
Now supplying most of Dublin's leading hotels, restaurants and
multiples with her wares, she divides herself between the
business and her five-year-old son, Charles.*

This coming December as the new millennium dawns and fire-
works explode, bouncing off the stratosphere, lighting up the
Earth like some giant Catherine wheel, I know that sitting out there
somewhere, perched on the edge of a star, glass of Guinness in hand,
will be my mum.

Two of her boys – HER boys, God she loved her boys, Danny and
Billy – will be either side of her, pointing out, explaining, laughing and
joking with her, not letting her miss the smallest spark or grandest
cacophony of colour.

She will be in Heaven.

She is in Heaven.

My mum died a year and a half ago. The doctors said she died of
Motor Neurone Disease. I know different. Oh, MND would have

claimed her all right, had she let it. But I know she died of a broken heart and an overdose of dignity.

She went through what no mother should ever have to go through. She watched not one, but two of HER boys die. Danny, her first born, died within weeks. Billy, her second and then number one son, died some five weeks before her of lung cancer. He never smoked.

Faced with the inevitable horrors and certainty of MND, my mum, Lily Frisby, decided to go and see HER boys.

I was one of ten, if you include Danny. Lily brought up nine children – fed us, clothed us, scolded us and above all loved us every minute of every day.

Lily minded us all to such a degree that in the winter she would get up extra early in order to set the fire and warm our clothes before we had to get dressed.

Lily adored making a fuss, but never being made a fuss of, except by her boys. She was a woman's woman. Glamorous in every respect.

Slight in stature, she always stood out in a crowd and radiated a warmth and understanding which inevitably meant that she ended up the centre of attention wherever she went.

What never failed to charm me in later years was her unending innocence and her enthusiasm to see and experience something new.

She loved travel, and would often go with Billy or me on holiday. Shortly before her death, the three of us went to see the memorial of flowers to Princess Diana.

She loved poker, and would spend a week in Wexford with her siblings every year, playing and laughing into the wee hours.

She won countless awards for Irish dancing and would occasionally have a cigarette, but never in the house, because her husband, my dad Michael, didn't smoke.

She wasn't a vain woman, but would never have been seen without her eyebrows. I made sure she had her eyebrows before she went to visit my brother Billy.

What I shall always miss about Mum, is my Mum, my Friend. Sure I still 'talk' to her. I tell her about my fears, joys, hopes and anxieties. When talking to my dad on the phone, I have to catch myself asking to speak to her. I still go to call her.

You see, she was always there, irrespective, unconditionally, and now, she isn't.

As the pain slowly passes, it is replaced with a feeling of privilege. Privilege that I had the best mum in the world.

Thanks Mum. I love you.

CONRAD GALLAGHER

Conrad Gallagher was born in Donegal in 1971. He has worked in some of the leading restaurants and hotels in the world – the Trump Plaza, the Waldorf Astoria and the Hotel Paris in Monte Carlo. After he was voted Best Irish Chef in New York, he was called to the White House in 1994 to advise on the St Patrick's Day menu. At the age of twenty-four he opened his first restaurant, Peacock Alley, in Dublin, which quickly won him a huge following.

I can trace the beginnings of my successful career as a chef and restaurateur to my early years of returning home and being greeted by the smells of fresh-baked bread and home-cooked meals – the smells of my mother's kitchen. From my early days, my mother taught me that dinner was not merely a meal, it was a gathering and a refuelling where, after a full day of scattered activity, the family would come together to share the positive experience of a healthy meal, and family interaction. It seemed that it was the action around the kitchen table that keep us together both physically and mentally, but it was actually the efforts of my mother, her determination to raise a happy and healthy family.

When I was able to see over the counter tops, I found myself by my mother's side (and sometimes under her feet!). She would, sometimes painfully, answer all of my why and how questions with as much detail as she could give. I learned that everything had to be done properly or it wasn't worth doing at all. A recipe was a chain of small individual events that created one big final product, and if just one small step was missed, it couldn't be completed.

As I gained confidence, it soon became me doing the cooking and my mother by my side asking the questions. It was then that I realised that I had learned the art of perfection, not from a perfectionist, but from a woman who loved her family.

I still take these early lessons with me into the kitchen, whether it be at home with my own family or in the kitchen of one of my restaurants. It is truly the basis of my success today.

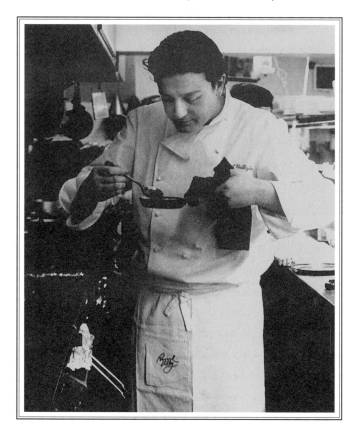

TONY GREGORY

Tony Gregory was elected to Dublin City Council in 1979, and re-elected at each local election over the last twenty years. He was first elected to the Dáil as TD for Dublin Central in 1982, and has been re-elected at each general election since then. He has been involved in many campaigns, including the defence of Dublin street traders (he was jailed for this in the mid-1980s), a campaign to expose heroin dealers and work for animal welfare.

People who identify Tony Gregory with Dublin's inner city may be surprised to discover that the most formative person in my own life originally came from a small town on the edge of the Bog of Allen in County Offaly.

My mother, Ellen Judge, was born and reared in rural poverty in the shadow of Croghan Hill, near the tiny village of Rhode. Growing up in a large family on a smallholding, she had no chance of realising her dream to become a schoolteacher.

When she was a mere sixteen years old, Ellen was forced by her family's circumstances to leave home and seek employment, like so many others from rural Ireland, in the capital city, Dublin. She found work as a waitress in hotels like Jury's and restaurants like the Paradiso.

The few shillings she earned helped her family back in Offaly to get through their most difficult years. The long hours and gruelling work took their toll and she fell ill with pleurisy in her teenage years, but she continued with her job simply to survive.

My mother did not marry until she was nearly forty years of age and then gave birth to two sons, myself and my brother Noel, the elder by two years.

My father, a casual labourer for the Dublin Port and Docks Board, was unemployed as often as he was in employment. Ellen filled the gaps by continuing her work as a waitress at night-time.

Her whole life was devoted to providing the best possible chance for her two children. She ensured that we would get the benefits of an education which she had been denied, and influenced both of us to become secondary school teachers, the aspiration which she had been unable to achieve for herself.

My mother's absolute belief in education as the only way out of a life of drudgery and disadvantage achieved her objective. Without that belief of hers, there would never have been an independent TD in Dublin Central.

Tragically, while my mother lived to see her two sons educated and in good jobs, the pleurisy of her earlier years and the hardship of her entire life resulted in recurring terms in the sanatorium in James Connolly Memorial Hospital where she died of TB in November 1969, when I was twenty-one years old.

My whole political life has been dominated by the belief that the deprivation and social inequality which my mother struggled against all her life, and which ultimately resulted in her untimely death, must be eliminated and that the aspiration of the 1916 Proclamation, 'to cherish all the children of the Nation', must be made a reality.

Tony Gregory

SEAMUS HEANEY

Born in Northern Ireland in 1939, Seamus Heaney has been a resident of Dublin for the past twenty-five years. His books include not only poetry, but also several volumes of criticism and translation. He has also edited anthologies and been a regular contributor to radio and television programmes in Britain and Ireland. He was awarded the Nobel Prize for Literature in 1995 for 'works of lyrical beauty and ethical depth'.

Sonnet III, from 'Clearances'

Polished linoleum shone there. Brass taps shone.
The china cups were very white and big –
An unchipped set with sugar bowl and jug.
The kettle whistled. Sandwich and teascone
Were present and correct. In case it run,
The butter must be kept out of the sun.
And don't be dropping crumbs. Don't tilt your chair.
Don't reach. Don't point. Don't make noise when you stir.

It is number 5, New Row, Land of the Dead,
Where grandfather is rising from his place
With spectacles pushed back on a clean bald head
To welcome a bewildered homing daughter
Before she even knocks. 'What's this? What's this?'
And they sit down in the shining room together.

When all the others were away at Mass
I was all hers as we peeled potatoes.
They broke the silence, let fall one by one
Like soldier weeping off the soldering iron:
Cold comforts set between us, things to share
Gleaming in a cold bucket of clean water.
And again, let fall. Little pleasant splashes
From each other's work would bring us to our senses.
So while the parish priest at her bedside
Went hammer and tongs at the prayers for the dying
And some were responding and some crying
I remembered her head bent towards my head,
Her breath in mine, our fluent dipping knives –
Never closer the whole rest of our lives.

Senator Mary Henry

*Mary Henry is an independent senator and medical practitioner.
She was elected to Seanad Éireann (The Upper House of the Irish
Parliament) in 1993 and re-elected in 1997. A graduate of
Trinity College, Dublin, in both English and Medicine, she has
been active in women's issues for many years, including the role
of women in civic life in Northern Ireland.*

My mother had bright green eyes and fair hair. As a small child,
people told me she was like a breath of spring, implying that I
would not even be a zephyr. She had modelled for a dress shop occasionally before she married. Once there was a photograph of her in the
Cork Examiner in a dress which showed her knees!

I was a sickly child. How she spent so much time singing to me and
reading stories, I do not know. Our house was built in the orchard of
another, much older house. My May birthday, she said, meant the blos-
som came out for me.

She was the best cook in the world. Home food was the nicest.
Some of her recipes seem to have been unique, hand-written in exercise
books. She made one cake with a crumbly pastry bake, then apricot jam
and, on the top, lightly beaten wash of egg with chopped walnuts in it.
This was baked and cut in slices. I have never met anyone else who
made this cake.

Ma was a great reader and encouraged us, but the level was fairly high. I will never like Dickens because I read him before I could understand his books. She, like so many Irish mothers, ensured we took schoolwork seriously and gave great support in time of stress.

When I was eleven, I entered for a scholarship for secondary school – there was no free education then. On exam day, with about forty other girls, I struggled through a terrible morning of arithmetic and Irish. My mother and some other mothers took their offspring to the café in the Savoy Cinema in Patrick Street for lunch. Papers were discussed and all except me seemed to have found them quite simple. I managed to tell Ma privately that I thought the whole thing was appalling. (The arithmetic paper was full of those questions about water running in a bath at such a rate and out at a slower rate, etc., and no-one around to turn off the taps.) 'Forget the morning,' she said. 'Your good subjects are this afternoon – English, history and geography. Have confidence in yourself – You will do well in them'. Would that all mothers would tell their children to forget what they had done badly and do better with what lies ahead. (By the way, I got the scholarship.)

All my life, she gave me this sort of support. She was my best canvasser for the Senate. I told her once how much I appreciated her support. She replied, 'But you were always very co-operative'! Only a mother could say that.

Ma was a wonderful grandmother to my children – she was the only grandparent they had. I phoned her every day for years; she was interested in everything. She died last year – my arm was around her – we were all with her and she opened her still-bright green eyes just before she died. Every day I think of things I would like to tell her – I hope she knows about them elsewhere.

Senator Mary Henry

MICHAEL D HIGGINS

Michael D Higgins is a Member of the Irish Parliament for the Labour Party. He is a former Minister for Culture and is also a human rights activist. In 1991 he was the first recipient of the McBride Peace Prize of the International Peace Bureau. Mr Higgins was a university lecturer for twenty years at the National University of Ireland, Galway, where he taught sociology and politics.

Dark Memories

Sitting in a dark room, she'd ask me
Not to turn on the light,
That her tears might not be seen.
We'd know it was like that
For, earlier she might have said,
If I was starting out again,
It's into a convent I'd have gone,
Away from all the trouble.
Or she would have spoken
Of lovely times in the shop, drinking
Tea and eating Marietta biscuits,
Or taking a walk with her little dog,
After playing the piano in the sitting-room

Over the shop, where soldiers came
And bought more biscuits, when life
Was easy in Liscarroll,
A garrison town; before my father
Blew up railway lines and courted his way
Into her affections.

She stood straight then, and, in a long leather coat,
After her mother died she packed her case
Left and joined him a full decade after
The Civil War. And she had loved him
In her way. Even when old Binchy placed a note
Behind the counter in his shop
In Charleville that when all this blackguardism
Was over, there would be no jobs
For Republicans in his firm, or anywhere else,
For that matter.

Now bent and leaning towards the fire,
With blackened fingers holding the tongs,
She poked the coals; and we knew
It best to leave her with her sorrow
For her lost life, the house she'd lost,
The anxious days and nights,
And all that might have been.

We ran outside and brought in turf
And did our lessons and vowed that we would listen
To what she said, of cities where always
There were voices for company, and churches
Close by, if never cheap.
We would listen to her story
And vow that, for her at least,
We, her children, would escape.

MICHAEL HOGAN

*Michael Hogan is Publisher at the Hoson Company, a company
which produces nineteen publications, ranging from the
Boyzone magazine to Magill, Ireland's political and current
affairs monthly. He began his career as a lighting technician in
RTÉ, before working in local radio sales for twelve years.*

My father died some six months before I was born, so my
mother, left alone with three small children, played the star-
ring role in shaping my life.

Our home was a modest three-storey affair in Athy, typical of
many towns, with an extension on the ground floor which provided a
sitting room and later an extended kitchen.

To make ends meet, Ma sublet a room on each floor as a bedsit and
so, until about the age of four, I shared a bedroom with my Ma and my
two sisters.

Most weekdays, Ma would rent out the sitting room to a number
of visiting professionals on a per-day basis. There was the Medical
Referee who came twice a month, the Optician once a week, the Chi-
ropodist once a week, etc. It was rare on weekdays that I or my sisters
would enter through the front hall of the house, as it would contain a
row of people queuing for the professional in the dining room.

My mother further supplemented this income with money earned from 'keeping books' for a number of local businesses. It is from her that I learned the not-inconsiderable skill of counting long columns of figures accurately and speedily without the aid of a calculator.

Ma was not a mean woman nor was she frugal, but she was sensible with money and knew the value of a pound. In my youth, I never wanted for anything, we were always well provided for in the fundamentals – luxuries you worked for yourself!

Ma also had an incredible capacity instinctively to assess character, which unfortunately, with the marked exception of my wife, Mari O'Leary, I have not been blessed with. Yet, I believe it's better to accept everybody at face value and be proven wrong, rather than have your judgement coloured by other people's observations.

My mother was an avid golfer and a particularly good one at that. She never passed the skill or the interest to me, although my sister Mary recently won Golfer of the Year in Rosses' Point.

Ma was and still is a formidable presence in my life, even though she died some years ago. She taught me fiscal rectitude, controlled risk, a willingness to forgive when slighted and a determination to survive against all odds, as she did on her own, never having remarried.

I take pride now in my sisters' success. Rita is on the senior nursing staff at Naas General Hospital and Mary is a senior insurance executive in Sligo.

I take great comfort from my own family, of Mari and the two boys, and often think how lonely it must have been in the early 1960s with three children under four, no nanny, no housekeeper, no running hot water and indeed no television.

My mother had been a housewife, a business woman, a cleaner, a bookkeeper and a million other things besides, but most of all she was and still is my Friend.

Michael Hogan

LORRAINE KEANE

Dublin-born Lorraine Keane is the second eldest in a family of seven children. Her career started on RTÉ Radio at the age of nineteen. She moved into television at the age of twenty-three and since that time has hosted live magazine shows and presented business and motor-sport programmes. In 1998, she took up the position of Entertainment and Fashion Correspondent for TV3, where she co-presents News 3.

My Mom – My Inspiration

I always looked up to you

Wanted to be like you from the time I was a little girl.

I remember watching you make people smile – you made them feel special.

You have a gift that touched people – You brought out the best in me.

I love remembering all those special moments we spent together.

When I was sick you would cuddle me, buy me a toy and a bottle of lucozade and try to make it all better.

I would hear you saying 'I wish it was me'.

You wanted to take the pain away.

You were there through all the special stages in my life: helping me to take my first step;

On my first day at school; preparing for my first big date.

Through all those difficult 'cheeky' teenage years, you gave me advice.

You were honest with me.

You listened to me – I could tell you everything.

You were my friend.

You trusted me and that was so important because I never wanted to let you down.

You taught me about the 'real world'.

You told me to respect myself or nobody else would.

You gave me a conscience.

Although sometimes it may seem that I don't need you as much as I did – don't ever think that!

You are just as important to me now as you always were.

You have helped me to be the independent woman that I am.

Your love has made me secure – It has given me confidence in 'Me' and what I have to offer.

You are my inspiration.

I hope I make you as proud, as you make me, Mom.

I love you,

Your daughter, Lorraine.

Lorraine Keane

CATHY KELLY

Dubliner Cathy Kelly works for Ireland's Sunday World
*newspaper as a columnist, feature writer and agony aunt. She's
also the author of two novels,* Woman to Woman *and* She's
The One, *both Irish number-one bestsellers, which have sold
around the world and are translated into six languages. She
currently lives in County Wicklow with her partner.*

Sitting on a grass-covered stone outside my grandmother's house, I'd wait for the sound of my parents' car trundling down the hill. Sometimes, one of the sheepdogs would sit with me, eager pink nose burrowing under my arm for attention, but even those ever loyal creatures couldn't figure out exactly what I was doing on the crumbling wall, peering eagerly right and left. Who knew which direction my parents would drive from? And I had to see them as soon as possible.

I haven't thought about those childhood vigils on the old wall for years, but when asked to write about my mother, that memory sprang instantly into my head. Friday evenings waiting anxiously for my mother. Summer spent in the beautiful West of Ireland countryside with my grandmother and godfather was a marvellous experience for a kid, but the torture was being apart from my mother. She was my best friend, my confidante, the person I couldn't live without. I ripped open her letters eagerly, loved the sound of her voice on the phone.

When she came from Dublin for the weekend with my father, I'd be in an agony of anticipation all week. I wanted to see the car as soon as I could, couldn't wait to hug her, talk to her, tell her everything.

Just being with her was magical. I loved to sit beside her and smell her perfume, watch her lovely hands with the pearly pink nail varnish she wore and listen to her voice.

She was everything that was good, kind and funny. I wanted to be just like her when I grew up. When she wanted a new apron, I blindly rushed to the shops with my ten-year-old's pocket money, bought two desperately cheap things and stuck them together with glue to make a 'proper' one. She was so pleased, you'd think I'd given her a diamond-studded apron.

Over the years, my mother has given me so much – love, support, strength and encouragement. And her sense of humour. At the age of nineteen, fresh from learning to type in journalism college, I decided to write a novel with Mum. Much hysteria ensued, especially because I couldn't read her writing and one of us kept changing the plot when the other person was out of the room. We abandoned any tricky bit by writing the words 'describe' in the margin. Needless to say, we didn't manage to finish our *War and Peace*. But we had so much fun doing it. Many years later, my first novel was published. It wasn't the bodice-ripping romance we'd hilariously tried to write together. But I wrote it determined to fulfil the promise we'd made then – to actually write a book. It was only fitting that I dedicated that first novel to my Mum.

The past few years have been difficult because of my father's tragic and slow illness but together, she and I have coped. It's made us closer than ever. I just hope I can be as good to her as she's always been to me.

Cathy Kelly

JEAN KENNEDY SMITH

Jean Kennedy Smith served as Ambassador to Ireland at the request of President Bill Clinton from June 1993 to September 1998. Prior to her appointment, she was active in Very Special Arts, an international organisation she founded in 1974 to provide opportunities in the creative arts for people with disabilities. Jean Kennedy Smith is the recipient of numerous awards and honorary degrees, and serves on several voluntary boards. In 1998, Ambassador Smith was awarded honorary Irish citizenship by President Mary McAleese, one of only seven people in Irish history to receive that distinction.

My mother, Rose Fitzgerald Kennedy, was the centre of our family, the centre of all our lives. She was the person to whom we ran for comfort as children, the person who understood us best and who guided us through the ups and downs. Mother was an inspiration – a woman of great faith, hope eternal, and boundless love. To her, motherhood was the highest calling of all. She once wrote that being a mother is 'fully as interesting and challenging as any honourable profession in the world'. She accepted that responsibility with courage, with humour and with grace.

People often remember my mother as a woman who, in the face of crushing sadness, demonstrated tremendous strength. I believe that strength was not given to her by chance. It was formed from her firm faith in God and her great love of life. Mother savoured every moment of every day – the laughter, the friendships, the delightful surprises. Together with my father, she taught us, first and foremost, to focus on the dignity and beauty of every human being. She taught us that love and generosity are the only paths to true happiness.

This lesson began in our home. My sister Rosemary was born with mental handicaps and Mother was faced with the unique challenge of raising a special child. Her response to that challenge was a wonderful example for me and my brothers and sisters.

As Mother wrote in her book *Times to Remember*: 'We decided that care, understanding and encouragement would be the way to bring out the best in Rosemary and develop her capacities to their fullest, whatever they turned out to be'.

Rosemary never felt ostracised, never felt alone in our family. Mother made it perfectly clear that from the moment of her birth, Rosemary was central to our lives. Through her example, Mother taught us that Rosemary was just like everyone else – that she had her own dreams, her own frustrations, her own interests and hobbies. Jack would take Rosemary out dancing and my sister Eunice would take her on trips. I was quite a bit younger, but I remember playing on the beach with Rosemary and laughing together.

Mother carried her love for Rosemary over to other children and adults with disabilities around the world. She became a pioneer in advocating the rights of people with special needs and, indeed, inspired all of her children to become actively involved in insuring equal opportunity and access for all.

In later years, my Mother would say that she was blessed with many children. Among them was a son who was President and a daughter who was mentally handicapped, and she didn't know of whom she was prouder.

Jean Kennedy Smith

As she once wrote: 'What could be more interesting for a woman than to watch one's very own child grow and develop, or more rewarding than to guide the child, with understanding, imagination, patience, perseverance, and to bring out the best that Nature has given? As I found out, each child is a continual surprise. Each baby is truly born to be different. None should be compared with another, for each has God-given potentialities.'

Brendan Kennelly

Brendan Kennelly has published over twenty books of poetry, two novels, four plays and a collection of critical essays. He is Professor of Modern Literature in Trinity College, Dublin.

She was smallish, dark, beautiful, a bit secretive. A nurse, she looked after many sick people in the village of Ballylongford, in North Kerry; she also looked after sick people from the outlying townlands. She had eight children, six boys and two girls. She baked bread every day for us, and kept us pretty well fed. When asked if she had a favourite, she replied, 'The one who is sick'.

She rarely left the house for a walk. She was always busy, always giving. Her life was an act of giving. She died of Parkinson's Disease. It ate away, slowly and implacably, at her body, and at her beautiful, pale face. I wrote this poem about her face when the Parkinson's Disease was ravaging her.

In the poem, I tried to capture the strange and wonderful mixture in her character of reticence, even secretiveness; of her ability to reach out from that reticence to help others in the village and throughout the parish; of her suffering and pain, her disintegration. In some people, a face is a map of the spirit. So I enclose her face.

A poem about my mother, entitled 'Her Face'.

The scrupulous and piercing hand of love
Wrote a few true lines into her face
Along the forehead, cheeks, about the eyes.
Her face was kind, or kind enough
To those who looked in it for hope and help
As if it were a holy well where men
And women came to stare into themselves,
To find the loving stranger buried deep within.
Her face drank pain, still offered its slow smile
As though the days were hungry and cried for bread,
As though itself, being lost, itself could save.
Her face sickened, either temple was a hole
Deep enough to contain the world's dead.
Her face broke in the grave, and is the grave.
O she is rich if she receives
The barest shred of what she gave.

PROFESSOR JOE LEE

Professor Joe Lee is Professor of History at University College, Cork, and is currently a Visiting Glucksman Professor of Irish Studies at New York University. A former member of the Irish Senate, his publications include Ireland 1912–1995: Politics and Society *(Cambridge University Press, 1989).*

My mother, Catherine Burke, the third of four children, was born of farming stock in Oughterard, County Galway, in 1916. Her mother fell victim to the Spanish flu in 1919, and although lovingly raised by an aunt, the loss of her own mother no doubt left her even more disposed to lavish on me, an only child, the maternal love that she herself can only have fleetingly known. As my father, a guard whom she married in 1940, was strongly supportive of her and me, I was fortunate to grow up in a totally nurturing home.

Castlegregory in the Dingle Peninsula, where my father was stationed, and where I spent my first ten years, was an oasis of simple if frugal pleasures for a child. But it could not provide a living. There were only two escape routes – emigration and education.

My mother's great passion was for my education. She herself had been denied entry to second level, having been turned away at the door of a secondary school to which she had eagerly tripped, not realising that one had to pay after leaving primary school. As she had loved school, the experience marked her life. Like many an Irish mother, and father too, of that generation, she transferred her frustrated aspirations from herself to her offspring.

That world is now so remote that a younger generation cannot even conceive of such harsh realities, as they take for granted the privileges for which earlier generations had to fight like starving dogs over a bone. Those parents who sacrificed and struggled to ensure their children could enjoy the opportunities denied to themselves are among the unsung heroes and heroines of twentieth-century Ireland. Their story has yet to be fully told.

Not only did my mother lose her own mother prematurely, she was also widowed prematurely, at the age of forty-five. The death of my father, whose memory she would cherish until she joined him in the grave more than thirty years later, left her desolate, although she was consoled by her intense religious faith, by the support of her extended family on all sides, by her joy in her grandchildren, and by the wonderful kindness of Sister Rose, Sister Marie, Sister Peter and the community of the Poor Servants of the Mother of God in Chapelizod. Their care, as loving as that which she had so often lavished herself, gave her solace in the face of terminal cancer.

To me, my mother, like my father, incarnates all that was best in 'traditional' Ireland. That Ireland is now going forever, for better and for worse. For all its injustices, from some of which my parents themselves suffered, the new Ireland would be a far better place if it had a fraction of their generosity of spirit. For, if to give and not to count the cost be the essence of greatness, my mother was a truly great woman. Every passing day makes me realise more and more how privileged I am to be her son.

Professor Joe Lee

Hugh Leonard

Hugh Leonard is a playwright.

According to my birth certificate, my mother was Annie Byrne. My father was a blue-black pen-stroke. Clutching at straws, because straws were all I have ever had, I reasoned that anyone who would formally sign her name 'Annie' instead of 'Anne' or 'Ann' was probably an untutored person. (When I first expressed this opinion in print, I received indignant letters from several well-tutored and articulate Annies!)

Ten days after I was born, a gardener's wife named Margaret Keyes took a tram from Dalkey into Dublin and returned home by another tram, this time with a bundle which substantially consisted of me. Adoption was a simple matter in November 1926; in fact, Margaret Keyes, who was imperious by nature, did not even consult her husband beforehand. She had had several children, all stillborn, and was forbidden to have another, on pain of probable death.

Mothers are traditionally supposed to be saints. My foster-mother was not. She had a drinking problem, although in terms of misery the problem was actually ours, my father's and mine. There were savage four-week binges that began at Christmas, Easter and Whit, when a well-intentioned neighbour would persuade her to have 'just the one for the time that's in it'. Almost to a paranoid degree, she was jealous of my unknown natural mother, who was portrayed to me as an ogress of the deepest dye. Childhood can be a time of terrors, and for me the most nightmarish of these was the threat that if I misbehaved, my 'real' mother would come to reclaim me.

My foster-mother was a simple, uneducated woman. On my father's wages – a pittance, even in the 1930s – she fed me, clothed me, gave me books to read, and took me to the pantomime in January, the Wicklow Regatta in August and the pictures all the year round. She probably spoiled me. She was too good a 'manager' ever to go hungry on my account, but we were poor enough for her to go without. When I won a four-year scholarship worth £240 – a fortune in those days – she could have taken the money; instead she insisted that I should have an education. Her thanks was that, like Dickens's Pip, I became a snob. I was a maverick in more senses than that of birth; as I grew older, the need for self-expression was pulling me away from the world of the Dalkey gardener and his wife. She was a possessive woman; her first instinct was to hang on to what was hers; a fiercer, more driving compulsion pushed me away, out into the world.

When I invited her to my first play, her tight-lipped, four word verdict was: 'Too much oul' talk!' She knew by instinct that the theatre was her rival and therefore her enemy, and, by an unspoken mutual consent, she never came to see another of my plays ... Her love may have been flawed and tormented, but it was also passionate, unqualified, selfless and total.

Comparisons, as Dogberry said, are odorous. A natural mother might, devastatingly, cite the superiority of blood. My own experience tells me that motherhood is far more than simple biology. In the climate of the 1930s, to be adopted was a dishonourable thing; only much later did I, with gratitude, realise that I had been one of the fortunates.

JOHNNY LOGAN

Johnny Logan is a singer and three times Eurovision winner.

Someone once asked me why I was born in Australia, and I remember answering 'Because I wanted to be near my mother', but it goes much deeper than that. I was one of five children, two born in London, two in Australia and one, my sister Fiona, born in Scotland. Liam, one of my younger brothers, died a week after being born. We were all tour babies, the children of the Irish tenor Patrick O'Hagan and Eily Gargan.

Mam was born and reared in Kilkenny, part of a large family, spoiled by all her brothers, very beautiful and very fiery. She met my father while working as a nurse in England – in Chelsea, to be exact. In the beginning, Mam supported Dad while he studied music, and then, as things improved, she toured with him. At the age of twenty-eight, Dad developed rheumatoid arthritis. Mam continued to tour with Dad, but from then on she dressed and looked after him. Never one to be very organised or on time, I think she almost drove Dad crazy sometimes, but they had a very strong love which held them together.

By the time my sister (the baby) arrived on the scene, Dad decided to buy a house in Ireland. Howth was beautiful and is still my mother's dream place to live. We lived there for almost eleven years, through good and bad times, while Dad toured for nine months of every year and Mam brought up four children. We were not quiet or shy children. No, we were always fighting, coming home covered in blood or disappearing for the whole day, swimming or playing football. Looking back, I don't know how she did it, being mother and father to us, showing us all an equal amount of love and care.

Sometimes it was like living in a madhouse, but always there was love. Mam was a big softy at heart. I remember the day she dropped the iron on our cat. She thought she had killed it. She called my brother Michael and they found some brandy to revive the poor cat. Mam poured a whole naggin into it. When the cat stood up, it began to sway from side to side. After two or three minutes we realised the poor animal was drunk. There was always something going on.

We moved to Drogheda in the early 1970s, where Dad bought a pub. Every weekend, Mam would sing in the lounge and always the same song, 'The Spinning Wheel'. I think it helped her to relive Kilkenny and her childhood. We stayed in Drogheda for five years, until Dad decided to move back to Australia. My younger brother Eamonn and sister Fiona moved back with them. I know this was very hard for Mam, because my older brother Michael and I decided to stay in Ireland, and in her eyes the family was breaking up.

We saw each other again several times over the next twenty years. I was with her when we buried Dad, and held her as I told her that her sister Bernie had passed away. I've flown her to Ireland four or five times to see her grandchildren and her family. On the last occasion, we travelled to Kilkenny to see where her mother and father were buried, and to party with friends and relatives. She always returns to Australia, torn between her family here and her family there.

Mam's life has not been easy. She was always uprooting and moving from country to country. She is now in her seventies, still beautiful, still fiery, still Mam. My brothers and sister and I love her very much and wouldn't change her. Sometimes when I'm on my own late at night I can still hear her singing 'Mellow the Moonlight'.

JOHN LONERGAN

John Lonergan was born in Bansha, County Tipperary, in 1947.
He joined the Irish Prison Service at Limerick in 1968. He was
appointed Governor of Mountjoy Prison, Dublin, in 1984. He
holds a strong belief that all prisoners are vulnerable human
beings and in need of our compassion and understanding.

My mother was born on 25 March 1913 at Ballydrehid, Cahir, County Tipperary. She was the third youngest in a family of nine – four boys and five girls. She was christened Bridget Peters. She attended the local national school and afterwards went to work on her parents' small farm. Three of her brothers emigrated to America in their late teens and two of her sisters crossed the Irish Sea to England. Incidentally, her aunt, Kate Peters, was aboard the *Titanic*, and drowned when it sank in 1912.

My mother also went to England for short periods in the 1930s, living with her sister Moll in Chester. On her return to Ireland she worked as a housekeeper for a family called Strappes in Clonmel. She always spoke very highly of them.

She married my father, Edmond Lonergan, in October 1943. She often spoke with great humour and wit when recalling their wedding day. The wedding itself took place at 8am, followed by breakfast, and the honeymoon consisted of a drive around the local countryside on a pony and trap. As children we often asked her about her 'exciting' honeymoon, and inevitably we got the most hilarious description of her trip on the trap.

She began married life on a small farm in the townland of Toureen, three miles west of Cahir. She had eight children – four boys and four girls, including twins. All the births took place at home with a neighbour filling the role of midwife.

We were poor and my mother had to work very hard to make ends meet. She was physically very strong and enjoyed wonderfully good health. Indeed, I never remember her being sick and confined to bed during my childhood. She did all the housework and much, much more. She carried water from the well, she washed all our clothes by hand, she baked the bread, she cooked all our meals, she knitted socks and jumpers and she darned our clothes. Most of her work had a big element of drudgery attached to it. She knew this too, and she often told us that she was our slave.

She seldom socialised – in those days only the gentry did that sort of thing. My mother's only outings were when she occasionally went into Cahir (the local town) to shop or when she went to Mass on Sundays. However, she used to visit three neighbouring families – Bretts, Bourkes and O'Donnells. As small children, we usually accompanied her on these visits and they were so often the highlights of our young lives. She never went on holidays and believe it or not, I never remember her being out of the house overnight.

My mother was our home – I could not even imagine it without her. She was kind and loving when it was needed; she was supportive when support was required; she was strict when discipline was appropriate but above all she was great craic. Like many of her era, she had a wonderful memory and was also a bit of a historian. Certainly, she enriched us with all the local history and much folklore and the odd sprinkle of gossip!

Finally, she was scrupulously honest, generous to a fault and possessed a great sense of humour flavoured with a sharp wit. There was never a dull moment when she was centre stage.

She died on 4 February 1991.

JIMMY MAGEE

Jimmy Magee has been a Sports Broadcaster for the last forty years. His work as a sports commentator has taken him to seventy-five different countries around the world in his coverage of eight Olympic Games, eight World Cup Finals and the US Open Golf Tournaments. During his career, he devised the questions for fifteen series of Matchplay *on Irish radio and also for the* Know Your Sport *quiz on RTÉ television. Known in Ireland as the 'Memory Man', Jimmy Magee is renowned for his vast knowledge of sports history.*

Rose Mackin was a beautiful girl. No wonder that Paddy Magee wooed her, fell in love with her and married her.

That was New York, USA, in the 1930s, at the end of which decade the new Mr & Mrs Magee decided to return to Ireland, with baby Jimmy in tow. Growing up during the war years must have been tough. Yet one was cushioned and protected by a mother who made light of the difficulties – no fuel except some wet turf, no white bread, no fruits, little oil and little money. It was wartime and rationing.

No more than a dozen years after they'd come home from America my father died. Mother was left to manage three children and a house without any visible means of support.

Often she must have been sad but she never showed it – if she was vexed she didn't allow it flow over my sisters and me. Though I was but a youngster I did appreciate her efforts and what I now, all these years later, recognise as expertise. The death of my father caused a reshuffle of my education plans. Long-term college gave way to the stark reality of getting out in the workplace and becoming *de facto* 'head of the house'. How often I thought that this lovely woman deserved better. She loved to talk of travel, but seldom got the opportunity. America was close to her heart. She could fire one's imagination with her stories of Broadway, Long Island, upstate New York, magical Manhattan. It was no surprise, when her children were grown up and running their own lives, that she returned to live in the USA.

When she was resident in New York, she yearned for Ireland. Almost a story of divided loyalties. But her final wish proved there truly never was a real division. Her heart always was where now her body rests in peace, at the foot of the Cooley Mountains, where once she roamed as a girl.

Writing these few words has brought sadness, in recall. How I regret that I wasn't able to do more for her. To bring her on a world trip, so that she could see the wondrous places about which she filled my formative years with the desire to travel.

When I finally could have afforded it, her health was failing, and like a lot of things in life, time was running out. Writing this short article has served me well. It has given me a public opportunity to pay tribute to a beautiful young Irish girl who emigrated, like thousands before and since.

A woman gentle, kind and smiling, who could sing a song in tune, and dance a dance in time. A woman whose faith was so unshakeable that she can obviously read these few lines now from her lofty perch. Thanks Mam.

NELL McCAFFERTY

Nell McCafferty was born in the bed of her parents in the Bogside, Derry, in 1944. She was a founder member of the Civil Rights Movement in the North in 1968, and of the Irishwomen's Liberation Movement in the South in 1970. A journalist with the Sunday Tribune, *she is an award-winning broadcaster and author of several books published by Attic Press, Dublin. She is coping with menopause and hot flushes without the aid of drugs.*

After each of her six surviving children presented my mother with their first week's wages – and were bathed in her pride and thanks – she always repeated the mantra: 'I have a passport for the United States upstairs in the wardrobe.' We used to giggle at the inference that a full-time mother had dreams of her own – of travel, freedom and financial independence. It never occurred to us that she even had a life of her own before motherhood.

She acquired the passport in her teens, in the 1920s, intent on following her older sisters and brother to Shangri-la. Her own mother died in childbirth, weeks later, and she had to remain in Derry, assuming, without question, the role of housekeeper to her father, and surrogate mother to her young brothers and sisters.

It was not until I joined the Irishwomen's Liberation Movement, in 1971, that I appreciated the significance of my mother's defiant, wistful, mantra: that she too coulda' been somebody – that she had, rather, an identity beyond that limited one socially ascribed and prescribed to her of 'mammy'. For instance, on Bloody Sunday, it was to her house in the Bogside that politicians and press made their way to take accurate readings from her of the political compass. She was – and is – a truthful, accurate *Passionara*.

After my father died in 1978, she renewed her passport and took off to Jerusalem and Rome. Her analysis of the confusion attending the actual site of the death of Christ is that a person never knows the real truth of anything. Of Rome, my mother regrets that she did not have the opportunity to question the Pope personally about the right to abortion after rape (she believes he'd make an exception in that case after conversing with her).

For all that I am glad and privileged to have been a daughter of the last of the full-time mothers, I am achingly aware of the sacrifice she made for the sake of her younger siblings and for us, her children.

In the mind's eye, I will always see her poised in her apron in the doorway between the kitchen and the scullery, wooden spoon held aloft, one ankle propped behind the other, laughing in advance of her own witticisms about the great issues of the day. I have savoured and repeated, for days afterward, her tales and observations. I hope I will remember them, in the certain days to come when she embraces death.

My mother was born on 10 November 1910. Her sight has failed her now, February 1999. The last book my mother read was *Their Eyes were Watching God*, by Zara Neale Hurston, the black feminist writer from Harlem, New York.

Of the second Christian millennium, to which she, at the great age of eighty-nine, teasingly refers as the 'Melodeon', she has this to say: There can be no Second Coming because a child can only be born once to any woman.

It should also be said, because these things matter in a civilised society, that my mother, in the days of her health and strength, was a baker and cook of excellence. Also, she knows the words of every song she sings. Do I love her? Jaysus, reader, she was and is the first love of my life, the touchstone by which I have subconsciously measured all others. I gather, from studies of Freud, that in this I was a lucky child: yes, I actually like my own mother.

MICK McCARTHY

Mick McCarthy is the manager of the Irish National Soccer Team. He has played fifty-seven times for Ireland at the senior level. Mick is married to Fiona, and they have three children – Anna, Katie and Michael.

How do you assess what your mother means to you and your family? Especially during your formative years. Dad's away doing twelve-hour shifts and Mum does everything for the four of us – John, Michael, Kevin and our sister, Catherine.

From waking us up for school and seeing we have breakfast before we leave, to chasing us off to bed, only after we've stretched our bedtime by an extra few minutes. She is on call to all of us. Always a loving and caring mum.

There, whenever we needed support or encouragement; on hand with advice and an open minded view, whatever the subject. A hug and a cuddle always felt great with Mum and made any difficulties or problems we might have seem to fade away.

It's amazing how much we depended on Mum. Despite the fact that she was kept so busy by four growing, demanding children, she worked as well. I wonder now how she managed to do all she did. The cooking, cleaning, tidying the house, tending and caring for us, and of course, Charlie, our dad. There were always cakes, pies, tarts and scones aplenty. Mum loved to bake for us – mind you, it never lasted long because we all loved her baking.

Mum was the focal point in the home and did just about everything for us, and did it unconditionally. Mum was loved by all who knew her – so kind and generous, compassionate and loving and always seeing the best in others.

A really lovely person, and I can see that so clearly now. Sadly, Mum died fifteen years ago of breast cancer after suffering greatly for a long time.

A desperately sad time for all of us, and we all still think of her and miss her so much.

But writing this has made me think about Mum more, and the saddest thing about Mum's death is the fact that we could all have learned so much from her, now that we are old enough to listen and appreciate what she said.

Mum would have loved to see her eight grandchildren growing up, and they would all have adored her. And of course for my dad, who without saying so misses her so much, life would be a whole lot better, as it would for all of us, if Mum was still alive.

At Mum's funeral the priest, who was new to our parish, referred to her as Rosie. It was a slip of the tongue, her name was Josie.

But I think it was appropriate really, because while Mum was alive all our lives were Rosie.

God bless her.

THE McCOLE FAMILY

Bridget McCole was a very special woman. A loving mother to twelve children in her native County Donegal, and a woman committed to seeking justice for the very serious health injury she suffered when she was infected with a Hepatitis C-contaminated blood product in 1977. One of the Irish Anti-D mothers, she took on the first High Court action to break the wall of secrecy surrounding the contamination, and received the first legal admission of liability. Her memory is very special to her family and also to all those who received infected Anti-D.

A Tribute to our mother, Bridget Ellen McCole:

One of the legacies our mother left us was to have the courage of our convictions and the knowledge that the truth could move mountains, as move mountains it did.

We all miss our mother dreadfully – she left a huge void in our lives, but she also left us many happy memories. Our mother had a great love for life, and a kind heart. She put a lot of time and energy into raising her large family of six boys and six girls. Her family was her life; we had a wonderful childhood, being raised in the hills of Donegal. I remember going to church on a Sunday after Mum would spend the morning getting us ready. We were all steps and stairs. We would take up a whole seat in the church, with Mum at one end and Dad at the other. She used to be so proud of her family. We also remember the mornings she would have all our school uniforms ready, from the eldest to the youngest.

Our home used to be full of laughter, as she watched us grow. Sometimes it seemed that our house would burst at the seams, especially on a Friday night when all our friends would gather. They also loved our mum dearly, and she would ferry us all back and forth to the disco. That's why it was so hard to accept when she started to become ill and when, over the years, it got worse and worse. She couldn't do the things she used to, but she tried so hard to be the same. She never let her illness be a burden to us, she coped with it. She tried going to doctors, but nobody could find anything wrong. It felt as if they all began to believe that it was all in her head. It is impossible to describe the pain and suffering mum went through, especially in her last couple of years, as it's still too painful a memory. When she found out the cause of her illness (hepatitis C) and the circumstances surrounding it, she had two simple questions to ask – How? and Why? She never wavered in her quest for the truth. She chose a tough path; she could have accepted money and gone quietly away. But as sick as she was, she didn't, and that is what people never understood. This wasn't about money; they robbed her and her family of her life and how it should have been. But she wouldn't allow them or her illness to break her spirit. They could never take that from her.

She always taught us to stand up for what you believe in, and not to accept anything less. She taught us to believe in ourselves and our dreams. Sadly, it took her death for the truth to unfold, a high price to pay. She was robbed of her life at fifty-four.

Our hearts are empty now but we will never forget her, for she was a Mum in a million.

On a last note, we would like to thank the Committee of Positive

The McCole Family

Action for their help and support through all of this, especially Josephine Mahony, who became a very close personal friend of our mother and family. She was always there for her when Mum needed her, and for that we will always be grateful. Last but not least, we would like to thank her legal team.

The McCole Family

PAULINE MCLYNN

Pauline McLynn is best known as an actress. She was voted Top Television Comedy Actress at the British Comedy Awards in 1996 for her role as Mrs Doyle in the cult sitcom Father Ted. *She is also a broadcaster, with her own weekly radio show on Greater London Radio, the BBC station for London. Her first novel will be published in spring 2000.*

The old genes are a great man, housed in the double helix of DNA from the mammy and daddy, that go to make a person up. In my own case, I have inherited an unusual and distinctive skill from my mother, Sheila: it is the uncanny ability to dial a telephone number very late at night, with or without remembering the ensuing conversation the following day. And it doesn't matter how long or complicated the number is, nothing defeats us. That, and her hands. I once looked down at my own during a car journey and realised that I hold them crossed, one over the other, and resting on my legs, in exactly the same way as she does. And their shape is as close as 'get out'. But that's not all – I have a drawing she once did of my Grandmother May, framed and in pride of place in my living room, and she is sitting with *her* hands held in the same way.

It's difficult to write about my mother without gushing, although every mammy deserves plenty of gush. Ain't that always the way?

Mammies get the guff off you when you're young, and the gush only when you're older and have them worn to a frazzle with your antics. My own has shown her family a fantastic time over the years, with very few dull moments. We grew up in a house that was always full of books, chat and several relations attending UCG. And when she decided to go to college herself to study art, that was added to the wonderful equation. As a result we were quite cosmopolitan in our tastes, and had dinner in the evening ('like the aristocrats', according to one neighbour). It was the house that every kid on the block wanted to move into when they were growing up.

But it would be wrong, and impossible, to speak of my mother without mention of my father, Pádraig, her partner in crime. Pádraig and herself have known one another since they were fourteen. Now, nearly fifty years later, they are still pals. One of the greatest pleasures in life is to be brought with them on a Saturday drive. We sit in the cab of our transit van, and meander through the most beautiful countryside. My favourite trip is the awesome Doulough Pass in Mayo, down from Louisburg to Leenane, and then over through Maam and beyond. He stops at Maam Cross to buy her an ice-cream, no matter what the weather, and then treats us to a fabulous slap-up feed in Oughterard. And on those days, sitting between them in the van, I look down at my hands and I see that they mirror my mother's, and echo my grandmother's. And I make a mental note to play with the telephone later.

Pauline McLynn

LIZ MCMANUS

Liz McManus was born in Canada in 1947. Married with four children, she is an architect by profession. A member of the Labour Party, she was elected to Dáil Éireann in 1992 and was Minister for Housing and Urban Renewal in the Rainbow Government of 1994–1997. She is currently the Labour Party Spokesperson on Health. Liz McManus is an award-winning fiction writer. Her first novel, Acts of Subversion, *was nominated for the Irish Times/Aer Lingus Award.*

Extract from 'Dwelling Below the Skies':

Our last visit was to the school my mother had attended as a child. The headmaster, she told us, had a liking for homilies about the wonders of nature. To see its ruined buildings, derelict and overgrown, must have been hard for her and yet her recollections were lively. Her memories swept throught the broken walls and along the exposed rafters like housemartins in summer. At one moment she stood in the corner of a classroom for punishment. At another she lifted her skirts to beat a way through the fields. Beyond the hazel trees a river slipped by where she went swimming with the Minnis girls and her best friend Sara McCracken.

Beside the school stood a Quaker Meeting House. It was a shabby building, crumbling a little with age, but clearly still in use. The interior was a square, timber-boarded room. At the rear ran a small gallery, lit by sunlight shining through the narrow windows. A smell of damp and old polish clung to the rows of pews, and on the lectern lay an open Bible. There was little else, nothing to relieve the severity of contemplation, and yet the tongue-and-grooved boards and the whitewashed walls gave the Meeting House a plain, homely quality.

'I always sat here …' my mother said. The expression on her face was serene as she sat down. Any pain or grief was washed out by the sunlight falling across her skin. Only the joy of remembrance remained. It was easy to imagine the rows of pews filled with children. I could hear the murmur of their voices drifting through the still air.

I can recall every detail of that moment – the light on her frail head; a hair snagged in the collar of her coat; her patent leather handbag slouched against the pew-end. Up through the layers of experience comes an explanation of sorts. What discovery was I making? The wellspring of existence or the disclosure of a Godly hand in the world?

Hardly. That is too simplistic a version of the truth. Full of contradictions, I have stumbled through life, swaying this way and that, under a burdensome, mongrel inheritance. You need to know where you are coming from, the proverb says, in order to know where you are going, but it is all a matter of guesswork in the end. When I see where the quarrel ends I will know my destination. In the meantime there are flashes of light, pinpoints in the dark to guide me through. Out of nowhere enlightenment comes, clothed in joyfulness and then, in the next breath, it is extinguished.

I don't know much. All I know is that there was a space for me among those phantom children. In that holy place, delineated by the absence of things, for a moment I belonged.

MOTHERS

MARJORIE MOWLAM

A member of the British Labour Party, Marjorie (Mo) Mowlam was opposition spokesperson on City and Corporate Affairs, held responsibility for Women and Public Service and Science in the Shadow Cabinet and was shadow Heritage Secretary before becoming shadow Northern Ireland Secretary in 1994. She was appointed Secretary of State for Northern Ireland by the British Prime Minister on 3 May 1997. She has been a key player in pushing the Northern Ireland Peace Process forward, resulting in the Good Friday Agreement and an overwhelming endorsement by the majority of the people in Northern Ireland through a referendum in May 1998.

My mother, Tina, has played an important role in my life. She has always worked hard, both at home and in her job. She had three children – I am the middle one. She is now in her seventies and takes just the same interest in the activities of her children and her six grandchildren as she did when I was at school.

She encouraged me to do what I wanted in life, and has always taken an active and supportive interest in my achievements and defeats. She is always there and certainly she is fiercely loyal to her family and friends. She follows events as reported in the media, collecting articles and photographs, and gets angry if she thinks I am getting unfair treatment from the press.

It's also good to have her views on what I am doing or not doing. I know that she is always straight with me – she will tell me if I look a mess on television, if my clothes or hair are not right. She also tells me if she thinks I am not making sense, when I am trying to explain some complicated decision I have taken about Northern Ireland.

Her realism and determination have taught me much. I think I have learnt from her and hopefully inherited some of her characteristics – most importantly, a persistence that keeps me going, whatever the odds and obstacles.

She agreed to be interviewed recently about me, even though she does not relish the limelight. I laughed when I read one of her comments about me. She said, 'Marjorie isn't that clever, she's just determined – bloody-minded and determined'. I wonder where I got it?

I hope my determination has helped people in Northern Ireland build a better future for their families and for the next generation. I do not want to see another mother suffer like Chrissie Quinn, with the tragic loss of her three little boys – Jason, Mark and Richard – who were brutally murdered on 12 July 1998 in Ballymoney. Sectarian violence has taken the lives of so many, and it is so often mothers who suffer the most through the pointless loss of their beloved children.

Marjorie Mowlam

SENATOR DAVID NORRIS

David Norris is a member of the Irish Senate, first elected in 1987. He is a member of the Foreign Affairs Committee of the Oireachtas (Irish National Parliament). He is also Chairman of the James Joyce Centre in North Great George's Street and Founder and Chairman of the North Great George's Street Preservation Society in Dublin.

Mothers are like children. Everyone thinks their own to be remarkable, and I conform to this pattern. I loved my mother and have no difficulty in saying so, even though I know that pop psychology sometimes suggests that a close relationship between mother and sons produces homosexuality. Well I don't think it did in my case, and I would not like to think that loving one's mother is just a gay phenomenon. She died more than thirty years ago and I am particularly pleased that even in those undemonstrative days, I somehow found the courage shortly before she died to tell her how much I loved her. I am also fortunate that her older sister survived and is still alive at one hundred – a remarkable woman who, although very different to my mother, has been absorbed into the role of a wise, generous and loving mother figure to me.

The first thing I remember about my mother is her wonderful natural gift for happiness, something which I have, I believe, in some measure inherited from her. Her life was not particularly easy. She was widowed when I was six and in those unregenerate days, while a widower received a housekeeper allowance, if a woman lost her husband, even though he might have been the sole breadwinner in the family, no similar provision was made. However, despite financial and family difficulties, my mother never lost her zest for life and her delight in laughter and music.

The first thing to go after my father's death was the car. My mother bought an upstairs model bicycle and used to sail off every morning on expeditions, either to the shops in Sandymount or to change her books in the RDS. The wicker basket on the front was capacious enough to carry a library book and small items of groceries, but in those days the two main shops in Sandymount, Findlaters and LeVerett and Fryes, telephoned for her order every morning and the supplies were then delivered in the afternoon by van.

Although we were supposed to call her Mother, my brother and myself universally referred to her as Ma. She was a natural and instinctive housewife and, although intellectually gifted, she found fulfilment in her home and family. She gave a regularity to our days which promised a security that, alas, was not to last. As I think back, the Proustian side of my memory is jogged by various senses. I can hear the thrumming of her old Hotpoint washing machine on Monday mornings. The sound of the lawnmower after I had gone to bed, or of a twig sweeping the concrete drive after a hedge had been clipped or new bedding plants put in, followed by the sound of the watering hose. She loved gardening and, as many women with difficult lives do, found peace and consolation in creating beauty in a suburban garden. Under the windows of the drawing room and study, she would plant night-scented stock and mignonette. Beneath the trees in the back garden, spring would disclose a carpet of daffodils, jonquils and narcissi. Often she would open the

French windows of the dining room and set breakfast in a splash of sunshine between the cooking apples and the plums. She was adept at bottling and preserving the produce of the garden, and our winters would be warmed by baked apple, cored, and flavoured with brown sugar and cloves, or the hot, tart taste of stewed plums.

She spent what I think must have been the happiest twenty years of her life in Central Africa with my father and while there she had two main hobbies. She loved animals and would coax them out of the forest, domesticate them and bring some of the rarer specimens home in her state room to present to the London Zoo. More importantly for us children, she also taught herself the furthest recesses and refinements of French haute cuisine. I have never eaten a *Charlotte Russe* as good as my mother's in any of the great hotels in the world. The creamy base would wobble deliciously as it was carried in with its palisade of *boudoir* biscuits and its crown of translucent jelly, through which glimmered the green of angelica, the blanch of almonds and the scarlet of *glacé* cherries.

There was a liturgical rotation about some of the meals. Easter would be marked by the ordering of a salmon from Sawyer's fish shop and so the arrival of spring would be saluted with salmon mayonnaise decorated with cucumber. Christmas saw the only time at which my brother and myself were invited to participate in the mysteries of the kitchen, when we were allowed to stir the Christmas pudding for luck.

She had a wicked sense of fun. I remember one Christmas when, having plucked and cleaned and cooked the turkey, she rescued one of its claws, stuck it on the end of a bamboo stick from the garden and, having tied nylon thread to the sinews, quietly poked it round the door. By pulling the string she made it clutch at my grandmother's hair. For one delicious moment, my grandmother's regal demeanour evaporated and she shrilled in terror. On more than one occasion, I also remember her using some valuable old family china and while we were all sitting at coffee over the remains of the meal, a loud crash and splintering could be heard from the kitchen. My grandmother, convinced that the Spode dinner service had at last gone the way of all flesh, rushed to the kitchen to find my mother happily dropping jam jars on the floor to create the desired effect.

Often my uncle would arrive from abroad for a few weeks leave and then another ritual was established. Everything in the house would cease at precisely eleven o'clock for coffee, shortbread and long conversations in French, calculated to arouse our infant curiosity and also to protect the secrets of the adults. When my uncle wasn't around, she used to go to meet her friend in Ferguson's in Rathmines or in Mitchell's or Bewleys on Grafton Street.

Not perhaps conventionally pretty, she had a noble face, full of humour and warmth. There were of course times when I disloyally wished she could have been a bit more glamorous like some of my friends' mothers, that she could have dyed her hair and backcombed it up into a fashionable American style, worn earrings or high-heeled shoes. But there was little chance of that; the shoes were certainly out since she was large-boned and crippled with rheumatoid arthritis. She also had an aristocratic disdain for the kind of cheap adornment I then thought sophisticated, but I think fondly of those long ago summer evenings when we lumbered together unglamorously up Simmonscourt Road to St Mary's Church for evensong or, if it was a weekday, to some concert or lecture in the RDS that had caught her notice. It was she who introduced me to classical music and even saved up money out of her pension to buy a piano (which I still have) on the instalment system, and lessons from one of Ireland's great piano teachers, the late Lily Huban.

Just as she laughed at life, she laughed at death and used to say that what she wanted on her tombstone was a verse that she had read of in a book, lines that had once adorned the grave of a busy housewife: 'Don't mourn for me now, don't mourn for me never, I am going to do nothing forever and ever.' However, when it came time to find some words to mark her resting place, I thought instead of words from the communion service which she loved and which carry in a more dignified manner the same message: 'The peace of God which passeth all understanding'. Although she is dead these thirty years I think of her often, and always with affection and gratitude.

Graham Norton

Graham Norton was born in Dublin in 1963, but did most of his growing up in Bandon, County Cork. Following several failed careers, he has ended up working as a comedian and broadcaster in the UK. He is probably best-known for his gratuitously rude chat show, So Graham Norton, *on Britain's Channel Four.*

Mothering Monday

It has always struck me that children are a bit like farts – people quite like their own. That little person sitting in a supermarket trolley seems to me to be nothing more than a screaming machine in clothes, with the added feature that it can also wet itself. And yet the person pushing the trolley can actually love the little pink ball of bawling. This we know – what is soon forgotten is that the love of a child for its mother is just as tough and just as beyond logic.

School was not a happy time for me. I'm not sure why. I had looked forward to it for months. Even at an early age, I had learned that there was a profound pleasure to be found in accessories. Pencils, a clean crisp jotter and a pristine shiny satchel sat in my room, heralding the day when a sophisticated, busy life would be mine.

Come the day itself, I began to have a slight nagging doubt. If this was such a great thing, why didn't my mother go? I really enjoyed all those coffee mornings and Bring and Buy sales that I attended. I was only four, but like one of those tiny table crumb Hoovers, I sucked up every scrap of gossip about 'poor so and so' whose husband was having a problem with drink, the neighbour of the friend who was suffering with horrible depression, and of course the deep awfulness of the woman who had a daughter who was going to marry a Catholic. I was too young to stay up for the Late Late Show but this Early Early version did me.

Upon arrival at school, I looked around at the sea of other children. Many blond, all cute and many with smarter-looking pencil cases than me. This wasn't right. This wasn't a special place that would make me feel special; it was a kiddie farm. I burst into tears and decided not to come back. However, Tuesday dawned and everyone was behaving as if I was heading off again. Short on arguments, I simply screamed. Like a piglet that had a waking vision of the abattoir, I was carried out to the car, but I refused to get in. Like a cat in a sock, I writhed around, fighting for my life. In the end my father, fearing he'd be late for work, had to drive off without me. I had won, but the victory didn't taste so sweet when I looked up at my mother. Her face took on the expression of someone in the middle ages being told that the world was round. The natural order of her universe had been turned upside-down. She lifted me and the dreaded wooden spoon up at the same time and walked out of the house. Few words were spoken. We walked quickly and I sensed that this wasn't really going my way. Sure enough, the streets began to look terribly familiar. I began to hang on to railings, doing my kitten in a sock impression once more, but my mother had something my father would never have – a wooden spoon. It stung across my legs and I found myself being herded into school like one of those calves I'd seen on *Mart and Market*. Nevertheless, it was an epic struggle. Two iron wills more tangled than a bag of wire hangers.

Now, as I stand in my own kitchen, stirring a pot of pasta with a wooden spoon, it seems so benign. It's a comforting tool, precisely because it reminds me of home, of my mother. Doubtless, some reading this would class my mother's behaviour as some sort of abuse, but for me it was just a blueprint for the bond between us. We would both do anything for each other and, of course, anything to get our own way. We are, in so many ways, peas in a pod, cut from the same cloth, farts in the night, and it all smells very sweet to me.

Graham Norton
123

EDNA O'BRIEN

Born in County Clare, Edna O'Brien studied pharmacy in Dublin before moving to England in 1958. Her first novel, The Country Girls, *was an immediate success, as was her second,* The Lonely Girl, *later filmed as* The Girl with Green Eyes. *As well as novels, Edna O'Brien has written short stories, plays and treatments for cinema.*

Extract from 'A Rose in the Heart of New York':

The food was what united them, eating off the same plate, using the same spoon, watching one another's chews, feeling the food as it went down the other's neck. The child was slow to crawl and slower still to walk, but it knew everything, it perceived everything. When it ate blancmange or junket, it was eating part of the lovely substance of its mother.

They were together, always together. If its mother went to the post office, the child stood in the middle of the drive praying until its mother returned safely. The child cut the ridges of four fingers along the edge of a razor blade that had been wedged upright in the wood of the dresser, and seeing these four deep, horizontal, identical slits, the mother took the poor fingers into her own mouth, to lessen the pain, and licked them to abolish the blood, and kept saying soft things until the child was stilled again.

Her mother's knuckles were her knuckles, her mother's veins were her veins, her mother's lap was a second heaven, her mother's forehead a copybook onto which she traced ABCD, her mother's body was a recess that she would wander inside forever and ever, a sepulchre growing deeper and deeper. When she saw other people, especially her older sister, she would simply wave from that safe place, she would not budge, would not be lured out. Her father took a hatchet to her mother and threatened that he would split open the head of her. The child watched through the kitchen window, because this debacle took place outdoors on a hillock under the three beech trees where the clothesline stretched, then sagged. The mother had been hanging out the four sheets washed that morning, two off each bed. The child was engaged in twisting her hair, looping it around bits of white rag, to form ringlets, decking herself in the kitchen mirror, and then every other minute running across to the window to reconnoitre, wondering what she ought to do, jumping up and down as if she had a pain, not knowing what to do, running back to the mirror, hoping that the terrible scene would pass, that the ground would open up and swallow her father, that the hatchet would turn into a magic wand, that her mother would come through the kitchen door and say 'Fear not,' that the travail would all be over.

The girl and her mother took walks on Sundays – they strolled, picked blackberries, consulted them for worms, made preserve, and slept side by side, entwined like twigs or the ends of the sugar tongs. When she wakened and found that her mother had got up and was already mixing meals for the hens or stirabout for the young pigs, she hurried down, carrying her clothes under her arm, and dressed in whatever spot she could feast on the sight of her mother most. Always an egg for breakfast. An egg a day and she would grow strong. Her mother never ate an egg but topped the girl's egg and fed her off the tarnished eggy spoon and gave her little sups of tea with which to wash it down.

She had her own mug, red enamel and with not a chip. The girl kept looking back as she went down the drive for school, and as time went on she mastered the knack of walking backward to be able to look all the longer, look at the aproned figure waving or holding up a potato pounder or a colander, or whatever happened to be in her hand.

ULICK O'CONNOR

Ulick O'Connor is a biographer, poet and playwright. He is best known in the first category for his acclaimed biography, Brendan Behan, *and his group biography,* Celtic Dawn, *about the Irish Literary renaissance. His play* Execution *broke the Abbey Theatre attendance record for a new play when it was produced in 1993, and this was followed by other record-breaking presentations, with* Joyicity *in 1991 and his one-man show on Brendan Behan which he performed himself. His translation of Baudelaire's* Les Fleurs du Mal *has been hailed as the best so far of the French writer's work.*

Requiem for a Nanny

> I saw from the water bus
> Like a dot on the piazza
> An old lady emerge
> From the gloom of San Giorgio
> It reminded me of you
> Who fifty years before
> Taught me the Stations of the Cross
> In our Church at Rathgar
>
> Taught me to 'salute'
> Priest – and person too

For you were from Tyrone
Where that was the thing to do.
Yes, I was brought up well
By Nanny, Ann Bell.

II
For you the Church of the Three Patrons
Was a temple of delight
Tented by that soaring roof
You made your own rite.
Loosed your mind from time to time
To join in the liturgy's swell.
The delicious strangeness of the Latin
Accept the discipline of the bell.
When in your ninetieth year
I took a chance and walked you down
(It didn't take a feather out of you
You wanted to walk home alone).
We went round the familiar altars
Murmured to the Little Flower
Touched the feet of St Anthony
Knelt for the Holy Hour.
It seemed like before except
That beside you I was the empty shell
Not feeling in that silent nave
The peace that enveloped you like a spell.

III
On my way out
I looked at the organ loft
Where Joyce's father met his wife
And thought of that devious poet.

But was careful not to mention it
Even in a passing phrase
For I knew you thought him responsible
For most of my wayward ways.

Ulick O'Connor

LIZ O'DONNELL

A law graduate, Liz O'Donnell is Minister of State at the Department of Foreign Affairs with responsibility for Overseas Development and Human Rights. She is a member of the Progressive Democrats party and was first elected to Dáil Éireann in 1992. Minister O'Donnell was a member of the Irish Government negotiating team in Northern Ireland, which negotiated the historic Good Friday Agreement. She is married, with two children.

When she was three, Carmel's little pudgy legs went from under her and she had a raging fever after a hot day at the seaside at Portmarnock. Polio was diagnosed. Her mother Liz, my grandmother, was distraught. There was an epidemic at the time and many people had been struck down. The family lived in the north inner city of Dublin, next to the Phoenix Park. My grandfather, John, was a quiet country man from Laois who had married Liz from the Liberties. She bore him six children. He drove a big black taxi; my sister Yvonne has toddler memories of eating Crunchies in the cab. One day, before I was born, he pulled into the kerb in Phibsboro and quietly died.

Carmel had a childhood of operations, hospitalisation and callipers. When she was twelve, she was hospitalised for a year, and denied visitors. At fourteen, hopelessly behind, she left school with a permanent disability. Her spirit was unaffected. She was a great beauty. Undaunted by her disfigured leg, she went on to play camogie with her other sisters at senior club level. She married my father, John, just after the war ended. He had been a handsome soldier and Irish champion athlete during what we in Ireland called the 'Emergency'. A job in the local Guinness brewery ensured that they remained in close proximity to my mother's extended family for many years. Then in 1968, out of the blue, my father was transferred to Limerick on promotion.

Carmel cried all the way to Portlaoise on the journey to Limerick; we children huddled in the back seat, convinced we were heading for rural perdition.

Deprived of the daily comfort of her mother and sisters, Carmel settled in badly. After many nights sobbing on the sofa, she slowly started to come round. She joined the ladies' club. She trained the junior camogie team; my father ran the sports and athletics. She regained her sense of humour. However, the death of her own mother, Liz, nearly killed her.

She has a wonderful turn of phrase; she talks to strangers; she has empathy. Sometimes when Dublin pantomimes came to Limerick on tour, she would laugh the loudest in the rural hall. The Dublin comedian would retort into the blackness, 'God bless you, missus'.

She was always on our side if we were in trouble. My friends envied us having a mum who wasn't 'stiff or starchy', judgemental or critical. You could discuss boyfriends or crushes with her. She took in lodgers to pay for extra things for us. The only investment was in us. My parents spent everything they earned on us. Neither was there any pressure on us about schoolwork. Our best was always fine. She loved us without conditions. She trusted us, even when I decided at seventeen to go to London and work instead of going to university. Later when I chucked in the safe job to go to university she supported that too.

Liz O'Donnell

She taught me everything important – values, compassion, style, humour, loyalty, hard work. She warned me about vanity. Whatever I did, she supported me.

She was first in when my babies were born. She stayed with us as new parents for weeks as we staggered through the sleepless nights of breastfeeding. A great believer in fresh air, she would whisk and wheel the baby out along the seafront at Sandymount and let me drift off to sleep between feeds.

When I was lunatic with fatigue trying to breastfeed my second child, she declared there was no medal for breastfeeding and gave him a bottle. She is a rock of sense. At election time, she moves in and ensures that my family functions.

She taught my children to walk, talk and potty train. She has secrets with them. So it goes on. My children draw from her as I do. She will be the 'making' of them, as she was of me.

EMER O'KELLY

Emer O'Kelly was born and grew up in Dublin, where she has worked for all of the major newspapers. She was a newscaster with RTÉ, on radio and television, for eighteen years, but left in December 1998 to concentrate on print journalism in the field of the arts and current affairs. For the past eight years, she has been the drama critic of the Sunday Independent, *Ireland's largest-selling broadsheet newspaper. She is a member of the Arts Council/An Chomhairle Ealaíon, a state body with responsibility for funding the arts throughout Ireland.*

My mother was just fifty when I was born; she was also fourteen years older than my father. I noticed neither when I was a child, since all children think their own situation is the norm. My parents' marriage was not successful, my mother having married at thirty-six because nobody else had asked her and she was looking for someone to support her, my father having married at twenty-two because he was looking for a replacement for his own mother who had died when he was three. Neither, looking back on it, seemed to have had a thought about what they could give the other.

Maybe that was why my mother never gave me any reason to believe that I was loved or that I had anywhere to turn for support. I lived in constant fear of her rages, never knowing when one would lead to my being thrashed. To this day, I don't know if it was a genuine antipathy to me as a developing little person, or because I represented the 'fruit' of her bad marriage. But then, she didn't really like anyone, except perhaps my sister and one of her own sisters. When I was old enough to understand, she told me that after I was born in my grandmother's house, and had to be removed to hospital for six weeks, she had been delighted, as it gave her time to look after herself and my much older sister. Neither of my parents, I was told with pride, visited me for the first six weeks of my life, and my mother was deeply resentful when the hospital insisted that she take me home.

I was constantly told how much I 'owed' my parents, and how I should be grateful for having such a good home. Not unnaturally, I developed a passion for reading, living in a dream world of convivial families and school jollity. My mother reacted by berating me for trying to be clever; she would 'cut me down to size', she promised. And she did. School prizedays were a nightmare for me – my parents were the only ones who never came, although they attended every bunfight in which my sister was involved.

My mother never tried to control her rages or hide them from us – I would lie shivering in bed listening to her screaming at my father. Her mantra on those occasions was, 'No, I'll NEVER be satisfied; never, never, never.' On calmer occasions, she used to offer me lifestyle advice: 'Give nothing to anyone, and take everything you get. That way you'll never go wrong'. After I had left home, my parents came to dinner one night, and my mother built up to one of her rages, which culminated in her throwing her full plate on the floor. In tears after she stormed out, I asked my father why she hated me. 'I don't know,' he said. 'She just did, from the day you were born.'

I resolved to be as unlike my mother as I could be; it was the only way she was a role model. But I never succeeded in breaking free; until the day she died five years ago, I strove for her approval, but never received it. When she died, I wept – not for her, but for her bitter, unhappy, wasted life. I also wept because now I would never succeed in making her love me.

Motherhood can leave a strange legacy.

DR AJF O'REILLY

Tony O'Reilly is Chairman and largest private shareholder
of the HJ Heinz Company, one of the world's leading food
processors. Born in Dublin in 1936, he is an honours graduate in
civil law, a solicitor and a PhD in agricultural marketing. He is
Chairman of Independent Newspapers, and also of Waterford
Wedgwood PLC. He is also principal shareholder in Arcon
International Resources PLC, a mining and Exploration
Company. A world-class sportsman, Dr O'Reilly played rugby for
Ireland twenty-nine times and for the British and Irish 'Lions'
team ten times. He is Chairman and co-founder of the Ireland
Funds, dedicated to raising funds to support programmes of
peace and reconciliation, arts and culture, education and
community development. He is married to Chryss Goulandris
and has six children.

My First and Most Enduring Love

My first and most enduring love was my mother. Being an only child, I was with her all the time, following her around, questioning her, being scolded and encouraged by her, and learning all the while. She was my perfect window on the world. Never again would the picture be so clear, the images so bright and optimistic. I loved her for it then, and I still do today. She was outstanding looking, quick to laugh, glamorous and one of a family of brothers and sisters who were handsome and adventurous.

Her brother Tony always said that 'Aileen was the pet of the family' – a family, I might add, of twelve children. He tells the story of being sent upstairs to read to her when she was a little girl with blond tresses. He would read a fairy story; she would feign sleep. He, having an urgent date, would creep noiselessly to the door, whereupon she would jump up and say, 'And what happened then?'

Rugby football has been such a big part of my life that it would be trite to say that she was my inspiration. But in truth, when you needed that last five yards to the line, I feel in my heart that it was her determination and singleness of purpose that pushed one to the ultimate. There is a wonderful picture of her striding past the old Gresham Hotel with me in tow in 1942. She had just convinced Fr O'Riordan, SJ, the headmaster of Junior School at Belvedere College that he absolutely needed a six-year-old at the school. But he protested, 'We do not take boys until they are eight.' She fluttered, I assume, her large eyes – and forsooth, I was a pupil at the ungodly age of six. *The Belvederian* of 1943 captured the poignancy of it with a photo and accompanying caption: 'Our only First Communicant.'

Again, she had triumphed over the code, and so it was at rugby. She took me almost daily to the small pitch at Jones's Road, where the great stadium of Croke Park stands today, and we watched countless little boys formlessly chase an oval ball with scant skill and wayward attention. One day she said to a scholastic who did not know her, 'Which one is the best?' He – Kevin Laheen, SJ – then uttered words which she never forgot: 'The red fellow's the best.' These were the last words I said to her as she died. Her great big eyes were trained on me – but somehow, she expected me to say it, and when I said it, she smiled and closed her eyes and died.

Perhaps the most unusual thing about her was her genius for friendship, and it was based on a very simple, rather primitive notion – that of giving. She never asked, she always gave – and often on very short commons. When we moved from Griffith Avenue to Santry, we were on the direct trade route to Dublin Airport. My football career had moved on to the international arena at this stage and on the morning after a match, I would bid all and sundry to 'drop in on your way to the airport'. They all did and usually ended up staying all day, but my mother could have victualled an army and caused a pioneer to blanch, and my friends left feeling the warmth of her welcome and the splendour of her cuisine.

Most of the intangible, good things, important things in life I learned from my mother. Kipling's 'Triumph and Disaster' were hers. A sense of purpose, a sense of patience and fairness, and a sense of gaiety encompassed her life. These will be my memories of her.

This will be her epitaph.

EMILY O'REILLY

*Emily O'Reilly is the former editor of Irish current affairs
monthly magazine* Magill. *She was also formerly Political Editor
of the* Sunday Business Post *and political correspondent with
the* Irish Press *newspaper. She is also the author of three
non-fiction books.*

It was sometime in the mid 1970s, when I was in my mid-teens, that my mother did something that I knew even then was an amazing act of love, not to mention a leap of faith, in her younger daughter.

I had been to a local disco and had met Derek. To fully appreciate Derek, you have to remember that this was the time when Glam Rock was in its heyday and Gary Glitter was a fashion icon.

To this day I can still see Derek – as indeed can my mother – clad in silver platform boots, tight denims, God knows what on top and a full head of dyed platinum hair. I thought he was to die for and as I strolled home arm-in-arm with this vision of beauty, I thought I was the coolest girl on the street.

My mother, as was her wont, had strolled out to the gate to see if I was on my way. God knows what went through the head of this Mountmellick-born, long-time Child of Mary member when she saw the yoke that her precious daughter was lugging home.

But she didn't bat an eyelid. With all the courtesy and grace more usually afforded to the local clergy, she told Derek that she was delighted to meet him and would he care to come in for a cup of tea?

It was an immensely caring and respectful thing to do, respectful that is of me and my adolescent feelings. She probably knew that Derek was going to be just one of a long list that was going to make that journey to her doorstep over the next decade, and that hopefully Glam Rock would be consigned to the popular culture scrap heap by the time I made my final choice.

It wasn't that she and my father had reared us in a liberal fashion. Far from it. They were both pretty strict, and my father thought nothing of coming looking for me in the car if he suspected that I was hanging out with boys somewhere after school.

But perhaps my mother, on that night, judged that I was old enough to make my own choices and my own mistakes and that I needed support and not censure – not even as much as a raised eyebrow – to allow me to do that.

To this day, my mother continues to be non-judgemental in relation to my personal and professional life. I know that when I had my first child she wasn't entirely confident that I was capable of caring for this tiny, wonderful little thing, but not for a second did she let on.

Now, four children later, I think I've got the hang of it and I also know that the lessons in loving that I got from her and from my father are the best things I have and the best things I can pass on to their grandchildren.

However, if any of my three girls EVER comes home with ...

Senator Feargal Quinn

Feargal Quinn is chief executive of Superquinn, a family-owned supermarket company which he founded in 1960. He is an independent member of the Senate, the upper house of parliament. He has been awarded honorary doctorates by Trinity College, Dublin, and by the National Council for Educational Awards. He received a papal knighthood in 1994. Senator Quinn is chairman of CIES, the Food Business Forum, and serves on the board of directors of the US-based Food Marketing Institute.

'I had the meanest mother in the world,' she said. The words caught the attention of the congregation at Mass in St Fintan's parish church in Sutton. It was Mother's Day 1998. The speaker was one of the parishioners, Ann O'Gara, who had been asked to speak from the pulpit by the Parish Priest, Father Ray Molony.

Ann went on to describe why her mother was mean. She had given her children healthy breakfasts when others got lollies. She had insisted on them having jobs to do at home when others got a lie-in. She had insisted on meeting (and vetting) their teenage friends when their pals could go out with anyone.

I recognised my own mother immediately. While my father was the businessman, the adventurer, the entrepreneur, my mother was the conservative, the maintainer, the protector of tradition.

My sister Eilagh and I were not spoiled – mainly because of our mother. Health foods, no early access to the cinemas, tasks to do at home. At six years of age my job was the fireplace – cleaning out the ashes each morning, cutting the sticks and setting the fires for easy lighting later. (Were there always three fireplaces to do each day or is that just my memory?)

Children very seldom think of their parents as romantics. We only learned much later in life how romantic our mother must have been. For more than forty-one years my mother and father were in love, and we lived in a home that shared it.

After my father died, a letter addressed to my mother was found in a safe in Newry. It was in my father's handwriting, with 'only to be opened in the event of my death' on the envelope. In case in contained something upsetting to my mother, I risked opening it and found the most romantic love letter I have ever read. It was from my father, written in the 1930s – about forty years previously.

She was a home-maker, and not just to her two children, but later to her ten grandchildren. She was also 'wee Mammy' to her nieces and nephews. This extended family – we have more than forty first cousins – may have been part of the Northern tradition. 'Wee' Mammy had been born in Colmcille, on the banks of Lough Neagh in County Armagh. She maintained that strong sense of family all her life. It is an inheritance that Eilagh and I value deeply.

Maureen Quinn (née Donnelly) died on 4 June 1979. A mean mother perhaps in some strict sense, but a traditional up-bringer whose commitment to her family home continues long after her.

PAT RABBITTE

Pat Rabbitte is Labour Party Spokesperson on Enterprise, Trade and Employment, and a former Irish Minister for Commerce, Science and Technology. A graduate in Arts and Law, he was formerly President of the Union of Students in Ireland, after which he worked as National Secretary of the country's largest trade union, SIPTU, before being elected to the Dáil in 1989.

My mother died from cancer when I was sixteen years old. I have never written that sentence before. The stark awfulness of its import hurts even now. I should have known the inevitable outcome of her illness that summer; but I didn't. You only have one mother, and whether by the law of averages or for purely intuitive reasons, you don't think that's going to happen to you. Modern psychobabble would have it that I am still in denial. Well, maybe. All I know for certain is that my mother has been dead for all of my adult life. I concede that it is easier to get on with life than to dwell on the depth of that loss.

One's memories therefore are necessarily childhood and happy ones. In the austere rural Ireland of the 1950s and early '60s, to have a returned 'Yank' for a mother introduced a slightly exotic note. My mother had spent almost ten years in the United States before returning on holidays and marrying my father. As a result, her horizons were somewhat wider than the typically insular outlook of the time.

Nor could she leave behind some of the strange foreign-sounding words and different customs and habits which we sought to imitate and relentlessly teased her about. She also brought tantalising images of a more glamorous but slightly intimidating world somewhere beyond the ocean. In an era when emigration was at its height and in a locality

where no household was untouched, it didn't seem to be any contest between American beaches and English building sites. And certainly none of the frequently returned building workers could cook as well as my mother!

In tenement Dublin, Sean O'Casey's mother characters struggled to keep the show on the road while their husbands played at being patriots. In rural Ireland, notwithstanding a paternalistic culture, the mother was no less the pivotal figure. Hers was the central influence on child rearing and education. In my own case, my mother had a profound influence in shaping my first tentative steps towards a life in politics. At a time and in a culture where fathers couldn't or wouldn't communicate with their sons, my mother always had words of encouragement and took pride in the achievements chalked up along the way.

To lose one's mother for reasons of incurable disease is a family tragedy. To see mothers die throughout the developing world because of malnutrition or inadequate maternal healthcare is a global obscenity. The urgency and scale of this challenge calls for the most intensive and concerted action among nations that has ever been achieved.

JOHN ROCHA

Born in Hong Kong of Chinese and Portuguese descent, John Rocha studied fashion in London. Using Irish linen in his graduation collection, he was inspired to visit Ireland. He eventually moved to Dublin, where he has lived for the past nineteen years, working closely with his wife and business partner, Odette. His clothing can be found in the best stores around the world and the John Rocha Crystal collections have proven to be a great success in the USA, Britain and Ireland.

My mother, Cecilia Lo, has always had the most terrific vision. Originally from mainland China, she chose to marry a man who neither read nor wrote Chinese (my father is Portuguese), going against all tradition, to marry for love.

Growing up in a small apartment in Hong Kong, one of seven children, I was always amazed at her even temper – I never once saw her angry or ill-tempered. Throughout my childhood, my grandmother lived with us, and later my brother's daughter also shared the apartment, so at one stage my mother was looking after four generations all at the same time.

My mum is slightly responsible for encouraging me to leave Hong Kong to chase my dreams. She formed a little community society to help raise the money for my air fare to London.

She is in her eighties now, and when I go home she is still as jolly as ever, playing mah jong, and listening to my father's jazz records.

My wife Odette says that if the sky fell down on my mum, she would think it was an extra blanket!

ALMA CARROLL RYAN

Alma Carroll Ryan is a well-known Irish singing personality who represented Ireland in the Eurovision Song Contest. Now retired, she devotes her time to her family and charity work.

Images caught between the crack of a door,
A five year old's memories:
Sleek, black, beautiful hair worn high,
As the scent of *Nivea Cream* brings me home.
Living your days with strength and pride –
That immeasurable power you possess,
Especially when you wore black or through a son's illness.
Wrapping colourful Christmas presents in November.
Pouring your heart and soul
Into each coloured bow and piece of Sellotape.
'Never again!' your motto, but never meant.
Sitting in the kitchen with Frank Sinatra.
Gallons of tea and sympathy
For life, loves and family.
Always with time for Charlie, Bill and Liverpool.

Alma Carroll Ryan

SHEAMUS SMITH

Sheamus Smith is the Official Film Censor, appointed by the Irish Government to classify all films and videos released in the Republic of Ireland. He was previously Managing Director of Ardmore Studios and an award-winning producer/director, working with RTÉ for fifteen years.

As I write this my mother, in her ninety-seventh year, is in decline. She may even have passed away before it is published.

My mother was one of a family of ten. Three of her sisters went to live in Dublin and became extremely successful in the pharmacy business, owning their own shops, but my mother decided to remain in Ballaghaderreen, County Roscommon, where she married my father. Together they ran a hardware shop and bar. Mother's abiding passion in life was her home and the welfare of her two children – my sister Muriel and myself. Our young lives seemed to be filled with long, hot summers; with endless days, due to double daylight saving time; with holidays to Strandhill, County Sligo; and with visits to our aunts in Dublin. Frequently, my mother would take me to see a film in the old Carlton cinema. Afterwards, we would often cross O'Connell Street to see another in the Savoy.

I well remember photographing my mother in our garden on my tenth birthday. In 1949, she decided to move the family to Dublin so that her children would have greater career opportunities. Unlike now, the west Midlands then offered little in this respect. Throughout schooling and my later career, and emigration to Canada and the United States, my mother was my greatest supporter. Her real ambition was that I should espouse a professional career as an engineer or doctor. Nevertheless, she understood and accepted my own decision to follow a different path. When I started work as a photographer in the *Evening Press* she provided, from limited resources, the funds to buy my first professional camera.

When my mother, finally and under protest, moved into the care of a nursing home early this year, my sister and I cleared out her home. One of her most prized possessions was a framed verse which I, as a child, had given her more than fifty years ago. It reads:

> Most of all the other beautiful things
> In life come in twos and threes,
> By dozens and hundreds –
> Plenty of Roses, Stars, Sunsets,
> Rainbows, Brothers and Sisters,
> Aunts and Cousins – but
> ONLY ONE MOTHER in
> All the wide world.
> Anon.

My mother, through her example, taught me the importance of generosity and, when I went to live away from home, the necessity of good food! Over my many jobs – in photography, newspapers, television and the film world – she followed my career and proudly read the credits on television programmes in which she might otherwise have had little interest.

Sheamus Smith

Even at the end of her days, my mother's concern is that her only son had never, in her opinion, been fortunate enough to have what she would regard as a proper job!

Margaret Smith died on March 3 1999.

DICK SPRING

A lawyer by profession, Dick Spring has been a member of Dáil Éireann since 1981. From 1982 to 1997 he was leader of the Irish Labour Party and served as Tánaiste (Deputy Prime Minister) in three coalition governments. He also held ministerial office in Justice, Energy, Environment and Foreign Affairs. Dick Spring has been centrally involved in Anglo-Irish developments over the past fifteen years, including the negotiation of the Anglo-Irish Agreement of 1985 and the Downing Street Declaration of 1993.

I welcome the opportunity to contribute to UNICEF's fundraising efforts for its safe motherhood programme. I'm also sure that if my late mother, Anne Spring, were alive she would be an enthusiastic supporter of this programme.

This project is about people, and the greater part of my mother's life was spent in assisting and helping people, from our family, neighbours and a wide circle of friends in Kerry and elsewhere. With boundless energy she combined the tasks of homemaking, raising six children and assisting my father's political career (in the era before PCs or secretaries). No task was ever too great, and she always seemed to be available to assist a neighbour who needed help or advice. The requests for assistance were as varied as they were numerous, ranging from driving an emigrating neighbour to Shannon Airport or Cobh, to utilising her nursing training to comfort a sick neighbour. On occasions when relations and old friends expressed views that they wished their children to attend schools in Tralee, accommodation was offered, despite the fact that there was already a family of eight in 19 Strand Street, Tralee. With all the comings and goings, our house was more like a railway station than anything else. My mother always seemed to be busy, yet she always had time for people, and especially time to listen when an understanding ear was required. In the course of an afternoon she was well able to supervise homework for numerous children, bake a quantity of apple pies (which earned her fame with our sporting friends), run up significant stitches in an Aran sweater and do a crossword without blinking.

She had bundles of energy, but then anybody who would cycle thirty-one miles from Killarney to Lixnaw on a Sunday to see her parents would have to! We have in our possession a collection of photos from her working days in Killarney, and there is a great vitality, energy and happiness reflected in many of those brown-and-white stills, produced by a humble box camera in the 1930s.

All in all, a very strong-minded person, one who was prepared to listen to a differing view, a great friend to have on your side and a formidable opponent, as many who tangled with her in the world of politics would testify. We feel very privileged as a family to have had her guidance and love for the greater part of her seventy-nine years.

Dick Spring
࿊

CAROLINE SWEETMAN STEPHENSON

Caroline Sweetman is the eldest twin daughter of Barbara Sweetman Fitzgerald, née Becker, and Michael Sweetman, who was killed in the Staines Air crash in 1972. Barbara remarried Alexis FitzGerald in 1974 and he died in 1985, leaving her twice widowed before she was fifty years of age. Barbara is currently Director of the Irish Association. Caroline is married to Architect Sam Stephenson, and they have two sons, Sebastian (7) and Zachary (4).

My Darling Mummy,

You have been a wonderful mother to me and I adore and admire you above all other women. Thank you for giving me a blissful childhood. I know now that I was very blessed to have had those happy, happy days.

You taught me about laughter, right and wrong, honesty and joy; taught me the importance of discipline in one's life; gave me a conscience and faith; taught me to fight; gave me comfort when I was worried and upset. Most of all, you taught me about love, your particular pure, all-encompassing, all-enduring love.

There have been many very hard and very difficult times in my life, but thanks to the firm foundation of my childhood, which you provided, I have survived.

I would like to apologise for all the pain I caused you and, looking back now, I realise with horror just how much I probably did. In fact, looking back now myself, I wonder how you coped at all and that you coped so well is the basis of my extreme admiration for you.

I remember so well the look of utter desolation and loss on your face when Daddy was killed in the plane crash. All your dreams were shattered, your world crumbled. You and Daddy were such a special couple, so much in love and so harmonious. I have no memory or sense of conflict between you.

And such a beautiful couple – you were thirty-five and he was thirty-six when he was killed. How wonderful you were to cope, being left with six children under fourteen. And we have all survived thanks to your quiet, patient, always loving influence. It often strikes me now that, despite all the terrible years, you have such a devoted family around you, with you as the central glue. And yet you have never demanded anything of us. It proves the saying, 'Love is free, and freely given comes back to you.'

One of the lovely and also annoying things about you is your modesty. You are such a giving person, yet you have no sense of how much people love you. I am constantly meeting people who have this huge admiration and affection for you. It is part of the enigma of you that everybody loves you, yet you do not realise it or the special quality that you have.

I am proud to introduce this dynamic, beautiful, elegant, gracious, intelligent young woman as my mother, more often mistaken for my sister; proud of you in your intensely hard-working professional life; proud of the way you have survived and overcome your pain, your loneliness, the hardships of your life. One of the things I most admire

Caroline Sweetman Stephenson

about you is how you have maintained your grace and love. In the face of all the hurt that you have experienced in your life, you have remained intact and without bitterness. It is such an example to me.

Thank you, my darling mother, for all that you have given me and for the privilege of being your daughter.

My love always.

Caroline

OLIVIA TRACEY

On graduating from UCD in 1982, Olivia Tracey's
original plans in the teaching profession soon changed. The
camera and the catwalk beckoned, giving her a successful
modelling career and her notable Miss Ireland reign in 1984,
a position which placed her firmly in the arena of national
celebrities. Television presenting followed, along with
commercials, product endorsements, fashion editing and image
consulting before she launched her acting career in Dublin's
Gaiety Theatre as Cinderella. She is remembered most especially
for her role as Lady Chatterley in the DH Lawrence classic Lady
Chatterley's Lover, *which attracted endless media attention. In*
1994, she moved to New York, playing Off-Broadway theatre, as
well as writing for the Irish Echo *and* Sunday Independent. *In*
1997 she moved to Los Angeles, where she pursues
both acting and writing.

After thirty-eight years as my mother's youngest daughter
It seems strange that I'm stuck for words,
However there is so much to say, and plenty to praise
That it's more of a beautiful blur.
And beautiful she is, both inside and out
Movie star looks with the aura of a queen,
The daughter of a presidential secretary,
Now a Tracey, but once a Keane.

Olivia Tracey

And keen were her many admirers,
Perhaps even to this day,
Yes, she could have been a princess,
But instead she chose her way
As a wife to Tom and mother to we five
Fulfilling her role with dedication and pride,
Always at the cooker to feed her troupe,
Delicious home cooking, from coconut scones to soup.
Mind you, I could have done without the stew
As it never was my taste,
But with the promise of dessert as the instant reward
I'd gobble it up in haste.
Come breakfast, dinner or tea,
She was there to do 'her job'
Providing Shredded Wheat with hot milk,
Followed by brown bread, or Kylemore Cob.
Then there were greens and fruit in abundance,
Year round salad and ham,
Now sparing me weight gain and dental bills,
Especially grateful for that I am.
Of course we were also allowed our portion of sweets,
Purple-wrapped Cadbury's in the main,
Along with tea and a selection of biscuits
But only 'one sweet, one plain'.
'Tomorrow is another day' she'd announce
As she sealed the lid on the tin,
'Everything in moderation' we'd hear,
And gluttony 'A Deadly Sin'.
Then we'd settle down to television
Only after the homework was done,
And she'd sit up straight, Lady Muck by the fire
Ready for entertainment and fun.

Olivia Tracey

164

She'd weep at the tear jerkers
And laugh at the funnies,
Especially at Benny Hill
As he chased his harem of bunnies.
But when caught she'd assume the regal pose,
"Disgraceful isn't it", she'd complain
As she tried to keep a serious face,
Stifling the giggles in vain.
As for Mom's moderation,
'Twas not shared by the Daddy,
He had a grá for the drink,
Alas, anything, from Hennessy to Paddy.
But mother stood by him, through thick and through thin,
'For better or for worse' was her line.
Then father got sense and left the drink in his wake
And now's thirty-two years on the dry.
As they approach their Fiftieth Anniversary,
A golden celebration in store,
Let's hope they make it a good one
And that they enjoy very many more.
Indeed I remember my own wedding,
'Twas asked 'Who's the lady in white?'
However it wasn't me they referred to,
But my mother, and indeed they were right.
Eternally elegant, thoroughly refined
Sipping tea from china delph
She's as simple as simplicity, noble as nobility
And as graceful as grace itself.

Olivia Tracey

PHILIP TREACY

Born in County Galway, Philip Treacy is now a world-famous milliner. An unconventional hat designer, he has been awarded British Accessory Designer of the Year five times since 1991.

Of all her children, I was the last person to speak to my mother before she died. I'd called her at home in County Galway from my studio in London a couple of hours earlier. She sounded happy to hear from me, and was thrilled that I liked the tee-shirt she'd chosen and sent me for my birthday.

Although a modest gift, its colour and individuality seemed to encapsulate the special bond that had always existed between mother and me – a relationship whose significance I sadly only truly discovered after her death, when I was twenty-six.

That alliance stemmed from our mutual love of beauty, whether in the nature surrounding our village life, in art, in human creativity or simply in the clothes my mother wore. As a child, it always appeared to me that Mother had a wardrobe full of beautiful clothes, but in fact we were financially poor and she had very few outfits. Her skill was in making the same clothes look stylish, year after year, by the imaginative adaptation of the few fineries she possessed.

Sunday provided the weekly highlight of our family life, based around church across the road. My five brothers and I were all altar boys and attended second Mass with Father, but Mother went with my sister to first Mass, making a special effort to look her most stylish for church, dressed in her very best clothes – and always 'set off' by a hat.

Like everything about her, the hats she wore were simple, but smart and striking. My most vivid memory of her hat-wearing was in her precise arrangement of the article, spending several minutes to ensure its perfect angle, making a humble item look elegant and sophisticated. However hurried, she would *never* just throw on a hat.

My fascination with beauty meant that I was always going to be different from the other boys in our family – something, I think, that bewildered Mother from the moment when, aged six, I asked her for some money to buy crochet cotton, having persuaded my form mistress to teach me how to sew and crochet. She was initially horrified but, after I'd produced what were relatively complex pieces, she seemed almost proud in showing my first efforts to astonished visitors.

Mother's prize possession was an old hand-turned sewing machine – an object which captivated me. So, when she went off to feed her hens after dinner, I would sneak the machine – which I could barely lift – to a quiet part of the house where, heart beating fast, I made my first illicit attempts to sew. Often, the loud whirring of the mechanism would bring her rushing in to snatch the machine away, fearful I was about to injure myself. But it did not stop me from producing designer dresses for my sister's naked, abandoned dolls.

She appeared to take this alien interest in her stride, although I felt her lack of open recognition signalled an inner confusion, perhaps even disappointment, about my unusual obsession. In contrast, her life comprised simple pleasures – tending her garden (which always bore a spectacular sea of colours and patterns), and looking after her 'girls' (the hens) and the geese – while tirelessly meeting the never-ending daily needs of her children.

Looking back, it seems fitting that I made my first hat, when I was eighteen, from goose feathers which she gave me. A Dublin lady bought it for the Races, and mother derived great pleasure, not from my first business success, but in knowing that one of her geese had gone to Royal Ascot.

Even later, after I'd won a scholarship to the Royal College of Art and my hats became popular, she observed my career from afar, never choosing to congratulate or flatter me. Amidst all the ensuing media attention, I felt the only person who didn't seem to notice, or see anything that was happening to me, was my mother.

Then, after she died five years ago, I found a scrap book containing all the articles about me from newspapers and magazines, which she'd neatly pasted in with obvious pride. It was heartbreaking to realise that, despite the physical distance between us, she had quietly noticed, and cared, all along.

At the moment of mother's death, I was working in my studio when a strange feeling of peaceful happiness and elation came over me. She continues to touch my life – and those of my brothers and sister – every day. She is bound to. After all, she made me what I am.

JOHN WATERS

John Waters is a journalist and writer.
He writes a weekly column for the Irish Times *and has*
published a number of books and plays. John is the father
of Roisín, who is three years old.

Some years ago, when my first book, *Jiving at the Crossroads*, was published, I found myself in the middle of a controversy, not so much on account of what was in the book, as what was not in it. Specifically, the accusation was made that my mother was no more than acknowledged in what purported to be an autobiographical work, and one which simultaneously lionised my father. This accusation was gradually extended until the impression was abroad among people who had not read the book, and indeed not a few who claimed to have done so, that I had 'written the women of Ireland out of history'.

My response at the time was simply to say that the book was not an autobiography. It was a story. But it was not the story of John Waters, or his family, or his town, or his time. It was most definitely not, as is generally held, the story of Seán Doherty, which I'll wager is a good deal more interesting than I would dare imagine. It was the story of a relationship between a father and son. As such, it drew on all that was necessary to sustain that story, but nothing else. My sisters were not in it. My girlfriends were not in it. But neither were any of my male friends. It did not attempt to write anyone in or out of history. In the writing of it, the story became itself and no more.

But there was another very simple reason why I have avoided writing about my mother. It is because my mother was, and is, alive. My father is dead. Indeed, my motivation in writing the book was, I now realise, fundamentally to do with grief for my father, who had died eighteen months before I started to write the book. Both my parents were, all their lives, extremely private people. I could not have dreamed of writing anything about my father while he was still alive, because the embarrassment of it would have killed him. As it was, I wrote only of what was good about him. His faults I leave for God. (Incidentally, one of my most virulent critics at that time has since gone on to make a considerable fortune out of posthumously destroying in print the reputations of both her parents. But this, of course, is art.)

My mother, like my father, has lived her life away from the public eye. There are few things that I can think of that I might do to her that would be worse than taking away her right to continue to do so. Once or twice, as a consequence of events in my minor public life, things have occurred which have threatened her privacy, and therefore also her peace of mind, and this has caused me more pain than anything that has been said about me.

She, for her part, has never ceased to amaze me by her capacity to ignore such assaults. 'Don't be annoying yourself', is all she says to me at times when I threaten to unleash the wrath of some powerful lobby, individual or institution in my – our – direction. But that is her stoicism, not her indifference.

My mother is a McGrath from Cloonyquin, and like her late husband, Thomas Waters, she is one of what John Healy called 'the great but anonymous people'. She likes it like that. Her Christian name is Ita.

For years, she was 'Mammy'; now she is 'Nana'. We all – my sisters, their men, their children and my own beautiful daughter Roisín – love Nana very much.

ACKNOWLEDGEMENTS

UNICEF would like to thank all of the contributors to this book who gave so generously of their time and thoughts. For many it proved a difficult task to write about such a personal subject and we are very grateful that they did.

Our special thanks to the Conrad International Hotel.

The O'Brien Press Ltd and UNICEF Ireland would like to thank the following for their kind co-operation and for permission to reproduce extracts:

Seamus Heaney 'Sonnet III' from *Clearances* by Seamus Heaney. Copyright © 1999 by Seamus Heaney. Reprinted by permission of Faber and Faber, London, and Farrar, Straus and Giroux Inc., New York.

Michael D Higgins and Salmon Publishing, Galway.

The trustees of the Estate of Patrick Kavanagh c/o Peter Fallon, Literary Agent, Loughcrew, Oldcastle, County Meath, Ireland.

Brendan Kennelly and Bloodaxe Books, Newcastle.

Edna O'Brien and Orion Publishing Group Ltd, London, and Weidenfeld and Nicolson, London, and Farrar, Straus and Giroux Inc., New York.

Cover: from (top left) *What Comes in Spring?* illustrated by Ed Young, Macintosh and Otis, Inc., New York; (top right) *Through the Window* by Tilly Willis, John Davis Fine Paintings/Bridgeman Art Library, London; (bottom right) *Baby Picking Daisies* by Dorothea Sharp, Private Collection/

Bridgeman Art Library, London; (bottom left) *Mother and Child* by Nguyen Tranh Binh, Galerie La Vong, Hong Kong.

We would also like to thank all the many contributors who supplied personal photographs and who went to so much trouble to help this UNICEF Ireland publishing project.